Solving Coyote Problems

OTHER BOOKS BY JOHN TROUT, JR.

Trailing Whitetails

Hunting Farmland Bucks

Nuisance Animals

The Complete Book of Wild Turkey Hunting

Guide to Finding Wounded Deer

Solving Coyote Problems

John Trout, Jr.

The Lyons Press

Guilford, Connecticut

An imprint of The Globe Pequot Press

NOTE: Before using any coyote-removal methods, consult state and local authorities to ascertain laws in your area. The tips and information provided here are not intended as replacements for professional advice. Some of the procedures described herein are best performed by a professional. The publisher and author cannot assume any responsibil-ity for any advice given here.

Library of Congress Cataloging-in-Publication Data

Trout, John, 1946–
    Solving coyote problems / John Trout, Jr.
        p.cm.
    Includes bibliographical references and index.
    ISBN 1-58574-400-X
    1. Coyote—Control—United States. 2. Coyote—Behavior—United States. I. Title.

SF810.7.C88 T76 2001
636.08'39—dc21

                                                        2001038366

To nine wonderful grandchildren—
Brittaney, Jessica, Mary, Sydney, Erin,
Allyson, Bradley, Emily, and Robbie
—and to those grandchildren who are yet to come into this world

Contents

Acknowledgments

This book has taken several months to complete, and required a great deal of research. Throughout the writing process, I contacted many folks by phone, fax, mail, and e-mail. Then there were numerous agencies that I just had to talk to without delay. I thank all for their contributions to this book.

I thank my publisher, The Lyons Press, and Jay Cassell, senior editor, for assisting me with this project. They have been a pleasure to work with—and, even better, gave me the chance to talk about the wily coyote that I have learned to respect and admire.

I thank each state and provincial wildlife agency for taking time out of its busy schedule to answer my one-page questionnaire. The answers these biologists provided, and the comments they included, granted valuable insight into the coyote.

A number of wildlife research biologists furnished me with articles they have compiled on damages associated with coyotes. These folks have certainly done their homework, and I appreciate them for taking the time to furnish me with these materials. I also appreciate the assistance I received from the U.S. Department of Agriculture (USDA) National Wildlife Research Center in Fort Collins, Colorado. In particular, I thank Russ Mason of the Wildlife Services facility at Logan, Utah. He answered a lot of questions and didn't mind responding to my numerous e-mail messages. I also appreciate the information supplied by many folks at other branches of the USDA Wildlife Services. There's a stack of coyote facts and data surrounding my desk that they supplied.

Dee Walmsley, nature writer, wrote the short story titled "Coyote in the Chicken Coop—Two Points of View." Thanks to Dee for giving me permission to reprint this interesting and entertaining piece, and for forwarding numerous bits of coyote-related information from time to time that helped this to be a better book. I also appreciate the help of her friend Kristine Lampa, who provided me with her master of science thesis on urban coyotes.

I thank all those individuals of Los Angeles County, Department of Agricultural Commissioner and Weights and Measures, for the statistics they provided about coyote attacks on and harassment of humans.

The Wildlife Society granted permission for me to use bits and pieces of some very informative research articles about coyotes. Its contribution is much appreciated.

I must say thanks to my sweet wife, Vikki, for sitting down in front of the computer to proof my text. She could have been doing something more entertaining, and she could have assigned me to the kitchen to clean up and wash dishes. She's always been there for me, and I will always remember that.

Finally, I thank God for allowing me to see and enjoy His perfect creations, from the landscapes I have admired to the creatures I have come to know and understand.

Introduction

When it comes to animals that share our domain, people have various opinions. Some animals we ridicule. Some we cherish. Then there are folks who really don't give a hoot. Usually, our thoughts are governed by past influences. Take the coyote, for instance. If one has hurt you or your valued possessions at one time or another, you may have formed a dislike of the entire species. On the other hand, if your only encounter with the coyote has been hearing one serenade the countryside at dusk on a cool, still evening, chances are you admire him. If you happen to be one of those who didn't realize that the coyote is a doglike animal that barks and howls, and is considered by most to be North America's number one predator, then you probably fall into the "don't give a hoot" category.

As for me, I might as well let the cat out of the bag before we go any further. Having been on both sides of the fence, I'm both friend and foe. As a landowner, I've suffered a few personal losses, and as a writer and researcher, I've discovered some pretty disgusting facts about the coyote that he would be embarrassed to admit. Now let's move to the other side of the fence: As a wildlife photographer, I've spent many hours along-

side coyotes, watching them do everything Mother Nature intended them to. This includes hunting for mice and other small
critters, howling to a moonlit sky, and sometimes just cuddling
and playing with their mates. And as an outdoorsman—camp-
ing, fishing, hunting, and doing other things that outdoor folks
do—I've had the fortunate opportunity to view the coyote at his
best moments, when he had no idea that I was there. Truly, he
has demonstrated to me his finely tuned predatory senses and
his place in North America. For this, I find the coyote a fascinat-
ing animal that deserves our utmost respect.

Nevertheless, here I am, writing a book that is going to provide you with countless ways to outsmart this wily canine. But if
you need to solve a coyote problem, this book is definitely the
right one for you. Maybe he ran off with your one-week-old kit-
ten in his mouth; or perhaps he has cut your sheep flock in half
during the last 90 days. Then again, maybe you have never had a
coyote problem. If not, I suggest you hold on to this book for future reference. More than likely you'll need it some day. You
see, the coyote really doesn't care how you feel about him when
it comes time to eat. He doesn't choose who he steals chickens
from, whose pet puppy he hauls into the woods, whose calf he
kills, whose watermelons he eats, and, well, enough said for
now. He causes far more problems than these, too, but make no
mistake: We'll get into the rest of them later. The point is, the
coyote could cause you a problem today, or tomorrow, regardless of where you live. You may be safe in downtown Los Angeles
or the suburbs of Milwaukee—or you might not. The coyote has
sneaked his way into many urban districts in recent years, and
you can count on being within reach of this sly predator in every
rural area of North America. But wherever you live, you should

know that he does his dirty work in two manners: (1) He may be secretive and do it only during dark hours; (2) he may do it in broad daylight and not care one way or another if anybody sees him.

Enough said about that. Before we go on, maybe I should come up with another name for the coyote. In all due respect, I'm not attempting to anthropomorphize an animal. On the contrary, in these pages he will remain the soulless coyote we all know. Nevertheless, you know how it is with a book. You have to come up with a synonym when you talk about one animal repeatedly.

We can't refer to the coyote as "Wile E. Coyote," because that name is a trademark of Warner Bros., Inc. Wile E. first appeared on screen in Road Runner cartoons in 1949. I'm sure you are familiar with Road Runner. He always wins and Wile E. always loses, even though the animated coyote invariably comes up with a strategic plan to outsmart Road Runner. But just for the heck of it, I did look up *wile* in the dictionary. It's a noun defined as "a deceitful stratagem or trick." Yep, Warner Bros. knew what it was doing when it named the Road Runner's would-be nemesis.

We can't use "Willy," either, because I have a friend with that name. He might not take kindly to me comparing him to an animal that has cost taxpayers millions of dollars. However, we could consider "Wily." Ah yes, we will drop the *e* in *Wile* and add a *y*. *Wily* is actually an adjective, but it becomes a noun as soon as we capitalize it. Moreover, after checking the books on my shelf, it seems that the name will fit perfectly. My dictionary defines *wily* as "full of wiles; sly." My thesaurus shows several appropriate synonyms, such as *acute, clever, crafty, cunning, shrewd,* and even *streetsmart* and *streetwise*. There are many more, but you get the picture.

When I first received word that I was the guy who would do this book, I began jotting down thoughts about Wily. They were added to a pile of other notes I had made over the years that reported both positive and negative thoughts about the coyote. Shortly after the book was assigned, though, I began to see the rest of the story. I would need to do plenty of research, and uncover every imaginable fact known to the human race about this amazing predator.

As have many other folks, I took the plunge and tried surfing the Internet to search for information; however, if you decide somewhere along the way that you need more information about Wily than this book offers, the Internet isn't necessarily the fastest way to gain the wisdom you seek. In fact, after pulling up a search engine and entering the word *coyote*, I came up with more than 42,000 matches. By the time you read this, that figure might have doubled.

I'm not really sure just how many of my matches would have provided information for this book. Had I decided to visit each site, my computer would be outdated and I would have downed a few 55-gallon drums of coffee. Interestingly, many of the Web sites I did visit had nothing at all to do with Wily. Sure, they referred to the coyote in one way or another, but many of these sites were not there to provide information and knowledge about the coyote as a predatory animal. Nonetheless, I did discover just how popular Wily has become in recent years. There is the Phoenix Coyotes hockey team Web site, where you can get the latest scores and team reports; the Coyote Book Shop, which specializes in mystery, suspense, and thriller books; and the Coyote Ridge Bed and Breakfast that offers a contemporary mountain home with rooms and private baths. There are thousands of others, including jewelry companies, parks, schools, ranches, and saloons, all of which are named after the coyote.

Perhaps the most useful information came from state and provincial wildlife divisions and numerous other agencies that, in one way or another, have had to deal with major issues involving Wily. These folks have come to know the coyote personally and are working hard today to know him better than they ever have before. They're the people who estimate wildlife populations, establish hunting regulations, provide wildlife viewing opportunities, and investigate all the many kinds of trouble that Wily gets himself into. The information these experts provided has made this book better.

If there's one point I must get across, it's that we must take the coyote seriously. It's okay to view the cartoon image lightheartedly, but once you turn off the tube you should head for the real world and see Wily as he really is. More than likely, he could catch a roadrunner if he so desired. However, he seldom, if ever, attempts to catch and eat a roadrunner.

Yes, the roadrunner (*Geococcyx californianus*) really exists. These white and brown, swift-running birds with long tails are found in many western states as far north as Colorado, and in Mexico. They prefer various types of habitat, from desert lands to mesquite groves. If you hear a roadrunner, he makes a *coo-coo* sound, not the *meep meep* of the cartoon bird. The roadrunner is also called the "chaparral bird." Interestingly, these birds will often incubate six or more eggs twice a year. They feed upon insects, various rodents, small snakes, and lizards, but if they have difficulty finding food, they may eat their young. Roadrunners also love to raid the nests of other animals, eating either the young- sters or eggs. They have a life span of about 10 years, thanks to their keen eyesight that often spots predators on ground and in the air. Foxes and hawks commonly prey on roadrunners, but coyotes seldom do, even though they share the same geographic region.

Coyote numbers are expanding at a rapid pace, and Wily has learned to adapt to habitat we never deemed possible. And of course, wherever he makes his home, Wily has to eat. That's not his fault. But make no mistake, if we are to coexist with him— and we must—then we must also adjust our own behaviors in or- der to protect our belongings.

Throughout this book, I will tell the story like it really is. As I've already said, I'm on both sides of the fence. I will always love old Wily, but sometimes he must be stopped. Someone once said, "If you can kill your own dog when necessary, you must love him." That's not to say that a troublemaking coyote should always be killed. Nevertheless, this book will provide you with lots of reasons to love 'em, and lots of reasons to hate 'em. It will discuss both nonlethal and lethal methods of dealing with a coyote when problems arise, and it will help you decide which method you should employ.

Dealing with a problem coyote is a controversial subject. There are several books about coyotes, but few provide informa- tion to help you to decide how to solve a problem caused by

Wily. You could say that leaves us with only opinions and hearsay. Some feel that eradication is the best and, sometimes, the only solution. Others say that extermination isn't necessary. Then there are those who claim we must focus on coexistence and forget about all methods of control. I'll avoid showing my sentiments and let you make that decision; however, I will say that in some cases we must attempt to control coyote numbers. Nonetheless, despite this need and this effort to do so, coyote populations have continued to expand into nearly every area of North America that we inhabit. Yep, it seems like the more coyotes we remove, the more they breed.

The coyote is a living, breathing allegory of Want. He is always hungry. He is always poor, out of luck and friendless. The meanest creatures despise him and even the fleas would desert him.
　　　　　　　　　—Mark Twain

Coyotes: Then and Now

QUESTION: Why do people have problems with coyotes today?

ANSWER: Because some people live in the wilderness, and the coyotes can get into their house and eat things and destroy things.
                    —Jessica Webster, age 12

In the cartoons we see a greedy coyote that gets everything that's coming to him—and some things that aren't. He's blown to smithereens, smashed by falling rocks, and run over by an occasional truck. I almost forgot—he also plunges off cliffs regularly. In the real world he has been shot, poisoned, trapped, scolded, and, on one occasion, slugged with a Mickey Mantle baseball bat. Despite this persecution, we should not necessarily consider Wily the underdog. He has survived the attacks of the cartoon world, and in the real world has expanded his territory dramatically in the past century.

Before getting into the coyote's expansion throughout North America, let's go back in time. Actually, Wily has been around since the Pleistocene epoch, which ranged from about 2 million years ago until about 11,000 years ago. This period is part of the Cenozoic era (known as the Age of Mammals), which is the most recent geological era; it encompasses the last 65 to 70 million years.

Some predators were even fortunate enough to survive the Cenzoic ice ages, and Wily was one of the lucky ones. With the increasing population of hoofed mammals and other herbivores that fed primarily on plants during the Cenozoic era, there was a need for predatory animals, such as the coyote. The earth could no longer rely on *Tyrannosaurus rex* to balance animal populations, because he, along with all the other dinosaurs, bit the big one about 60 million years earlier. That left the job to other predators, such as Wily. The early coyote probably looked nothing like he does today; but then again, the tigers, lions, wolves, and bears that also evolved from the Pleistocene epoch don't either.

Coyotes are members of the Canidae family, which includes dogs, foxes, wolves, and about four species of European jackals. You could say these other canids are the coyote's cousins. In 1833, Thomas Say coined the scientific name for coyote, *Canis latrans,* which means "barking dog"; however, the coyote's common name actually derives from the Aztec word *coyotl,* which reportedly means "trickster." Native Americans often called the coyote little wolf; in the northern United States and in Canada they're known as brush wolves. Members of the Lewis and Clark expedition called them prairie wolves. There are a few other pleasant names for the coyote, all of which seem to fit his culture, look-alikes, and habitats.

Coyote Facts

Common Name:	Coyote
Other Names:	Brush wolf, little wolf, prairie wolf, song dog
Aztec Name:	*Coyotl*
Class:	Mammalia
Order:	Carnivora
Family:	Canidae
Genus:	*Canis*
Species:	*latrans*
Other Canids Generalized:	Mutt, mongrel, wolf, fox
More Canids Generalized:	Coon dog, police dog, watchdog, house dog
Noncanids:	Hot dogs, chili dogs, corn dogs

How many subspecies of *Canis latrans* are there? That's a good question. During my research, I found more than one answer. Significant variations in size and color, which you'll read about in the following chapter, have led to the classification of fifteen to twenty-one subspecies. The discrepancy in numbers probably only goes back to recent times when coyotes began expanding their territory. For now, I will believe Hartly H. T. Jackson, a biologist who felt there were substantial differences among nineteen coyote subspecies. Yet to most folks, it really doesn't matter. All coyotes possess similar or, in some cases, identical habits.

About the time Christopher Columbus arrived in the New World, the coyote was limited to the North American plains, west from Kansas to the Rocky Mountains, as far south as northern Mexico, and as far north as Michigan, Minnesota, and Wisconsin. South of the Rockies, Wily roamed the dry deserts into the Baja California peninsula. He was just about anywhere where forests didn't exist. At one time we associated the coyote with only grasslands and prairies. Today we should associate him with any type of habitat, be it forest, plains, or asphalt.

When Europeans first began exploring North America, there was another great predator roaming the continent: the wolf. Established populations of *Canis niger*, or red wolf, were found throughout many areas of the South. Meanwhile, gray wolves (*C. lupus*), also known as timber wolves, held the position of primary predator in the northern portions of the continent. I might add, back then coyotes were part of the wolf's diet.

It didn't take long for humans to decimate wolf populations. As the years passed and settlers expanded their range, wolf numbers dropped drastically. Coyotes gained from the destruction of their enemy, taking advantage of fewer wolves to increase their own populations in the centuries that followed. Today wolves no longer rule over coyotes. Instead, the coyote has become the chief predator among canines. The fox ranks second.

As European settlers continued their move westward, coyotes inched eastward, northward, and southward. During this period, pioneers quickly became familiar with Wily and began naming creeks and other landmarks after him. There was even the "coyote house," which was simply an underground burrow covered with boards. Pioneers lived in these cellars while their houses were under construction. More than likely, they called them coyote houses because coyotes often dug holes to house their young.

The Apache also thought a lot of the coyote, enough to name groups in their tribe, on his behalf, "Coyoteros." The Dakota, Chinook, Flathead, Navajo, and other Indian tribes also associated their cultures with the coyote. There are reports of domesticated coyotes among some tribes, which probably came after pups were taken from dens. Obviously, Wily ranked as high on the popularity list then as he does today.

In the early 1900s wolf populations declined to all-time lows. Yet, the ecosystem's balance called for a predator. The stage was set and Wily promptly volunteered to expand his range, attempting to become North America's most abundant predator. After all, he had what it takes to do the job. He could now enter the forested regions where he once had feared the wolf. With the wolf nearly out of the picture, the only thing Wily needed to do was prove that he could survive in habitat different from what he was accustomed to during previous centuries. He had all the skills a predator needed, and he was a strong survivor, despite a price on his head.

Because of livestock losses reported by farmers and ranchers, the Missouri legislature passed a bounty law on coyotes and wolves in 1825. At that time coyotes primarily inhabited the prairie regions found in the northwestern portion of the state. The bounties reduced the number of wolves but did little to control the coyote population. By the 1950s coyote numbers had increased and spread to the southern and eastern parts of Missouri. By the end of the 1970s coyotes inhabited every portion of the state. As for the bounties, state funds were issued until 1968, although some counties continued to pay a small bounty for several more years.

Other states jumped to initiate bounty programs, too. North Dakota started one in the late 1800s. It wasn't long before Minnesota, Michigan, and others joined in. At one time more than 30 states paid bounties for killing one animal or another. Even provinces in Canada paid bounties for killing timber wolves and prairie wolves (coyotes). *The Clever Coyote* by Stanley P. Young and Hartley H. T. Jackson, published by the Wildlife Management Institute in 1951, included an official copy of bounty regulations from Alberta that showed that three dollars would be paid for each prairie wolf killed from April 1, 1946, to October 15, 1946. The successful bounty hunter had to answer a few questions and sign an affidavit to get paid, but only after he produced both ears intact with the pelt.

Nova Scotia initiated a bounty on coyotes as late as 1982. Successful bounty hunters were paid $50 for each coyote. Although the bounty program was eliminated in 1986, it did serve to provide the wildlife agency in the province with valuable reproduction data.

States and provinces have paid money to sportsmen and other concerned individuals to kill coyotes, numerous other predators, and starlings and pigeons that have caused problems. One thing we have learned from the bounties is that they do not necessarily reduce coyote populations, although millions of dollars have been paid in an effort to do so. In fact, Mother

Nature has done an outstanding job of producing coyotes faster than we have destroyed them. I believe any biologist will agree that bounties have not affected the population growth of the coyote.

As the twentieth century progressed, the coyote spread farther eastward across the Mississippi River. His expansion came with and without human help. For instance, Alabama claims that foxhunters introduced the coyote in the 1920s. The July 1929 edition of *Alabama Game and Fish News* reported coyotes killed in Barbour, Autauga, and Marengo Counties. In the northeastern United States, some folks believe that coyotes were brought into certain areas to eliminate the number of hares that were damaging shrubs and saplings, but this has not been proven as far as I know.

The coyote spread farther to the southeast and by the early 1970s had reached northwestern Florida. This was due to the predator's natural range expansion and from the reproduction of those that had been illegally trucked in from western states and released many years earlier. In Polk County, for instance, a local foxhunter who believed he was stocking a declining fox population brought coyotes into the state with the understanding he was getting animals known as "black foxes." Nevertheless, this incident probably makes little difference today. The coyote would have arrived there anyway, perhaps a few months or years later, as he has nearly everywhere else east of the Mississippi River.

Surprisingly, coyotes expanded into many areas without us knowing it. It wasn't something we could sit back and watch. It's just that one day, people claimed to have seen a coyote in an

Wily, curious, playful, devious—the coyote is one of the most adaptable animals in the world.

area where they hadn't been spotted previously. Some laughed at this claim, refusing to believe that Wily had arrived in their neighborhood. Today those who laughed have been forced to eat their words. I once read, "A coyote might live under your porch and you would never know it." Make no mistake—this writer knew what he was talking about. A coyote can sneak his way into a new habitat and may live there for a few years or even decades before most of us realize it.

A good possibility exists that some coyotes crossed the great rivers by way of automobile. You know how it works. Tourists visit the Grand Canyon or a western park, and stumble onto a coyote den. Then they look around to see if anybody is watching. If not, they snatch up a cute and cuddly western coyote pup, throw it in their car, and head home with a weird pet that their neighbors will look at in disbelief. Many such folks soon discovered, though, that once a coyote matures beyond the puppy stage, it becomes difficult to raise. Thus, some of these coyotes were released. Others probably escaped.

Some of these incidents occurred long before many states confirmed the presence of coyotes. Consider a few of these facts: A Maryland coyote was killed in 1922, but nobody knows how it got there. A coyote was taken in North Carolina during the fall of 1938 after killing about 100 chickens on one farm. Nine years earlier in Georgia, a coyote was captured and taken to a zoo.

Georgia officials say coyotes first appeared there in the early to mid-1900s. New York and Ohio believe theirs arrived in the early 1920s. Pennsylvania claims there were infrequent reports of coyotes in the 1920s, but reliable documentation of the presence of coyotes wasn't available until the 1930s. Farther to the northeast, Vermont places them in the state in the 1940s, and Connecticut says the first sightings occurred around 1950. They reached Alaska halfway through the nineteenth century. Some of the first sightings were reported on the mainland of southeast Alaska, but the population peak occurred in the 1940s. But unlike some states and provinces that have seen continuous growth of coyote numbers, populations declined in the state in recent decades. Today the highest densities of coyotes are found in the Kenai Peninsula, Matanuska-Susitna Valleys, and Copper River Valley.

In the Midwest, Illinois believes that coyote populations began establishing themselves soundly around 1950. South Carolina claims that coyotes were not recognized in the northwestern portion of the state until 1978. Indiana, Kentucky, Rhode Island, West Virginia, and several other states also estimate that the coyote entered the area sometime during the 1970s.

Coyotes set up home in Ontario, Canada, in the early 1900s, with populations increasing considerably in the late 1930s. Quebec and Manitoba claim they arrived in the 1940s. New Brunswick reports that coyotes arrived in 1965, while Nova Scotia places them in the province about 1975. By the mid-1940s, however, Alberta officials had already established a bounty on coyotes.

You can safely assume that coyotes did not roam entire states and provinces at the time the first sightings occurred. They may have inhabited one or two counties of a state, or only a small area of a certain province. Interestingly, coyotes now thrive in every area of some states and provinces, including the streets of suburbs and cities. In some areas the major expansion occurred during a 10- to 20-year span.

Strangely and a bit confusingly, coyote sightings in contiguous states have varied by several decades, even though it would seem they would have had to cross some states to get to others. The move of the coyote was primarily eastward. Yet, for instance, if coyotes inhabited Ohio in 1920, how could they not have been reported in other midwestern states until the 1970s? The answer probably rests upon habitat preferences as they moved eastward, availability of prey, just how long a coyote might have stuck around in a given area, and how they got there. You can also consider actual proof of existence. If someone saw a coyote 20 years before they were confirmed, this individual might have been placed in the same class with the guy up the road who saw a Martian saucer and two green men. The best answer I can offer is to refer back to the writer who said Wily can live under your porch without your knowing it.

You can also consider another factor: The eastern coyote is not the same animal as the western coyote. It's believed that there has been interbreeding of the prairie coyote of the West and the wolves of the Northeast. This is thought to have occurred in Ontario, Canada; in Maine; and in several other northeastern states. Although the two species of coyotes look alike, we find a larger coyote in the eastern United States and Canada than we do in the prairie lands of the West.

In all reality, most officials didn't confirm the existence of coyotes until concrete proof was produced. For instance, they might have found a specimen, such as a skull or an intact dead coyote. In other cases, hunters killed coyotes in areas where they hadn't previously been known to exist. Some believed they must have escaped from captivity or been released by someone just for the fun of it. For these reasons, though, I believe we should leave a little room for speculation when deciding just when the coyote first appeared in some areas. Wily probably arrived long before we knew it, perhaps some 10 or 20 years earlier, just before the neighbor's pretty little kitty disappeared one day. Today some folks will blame Wily for a kitty's disappearance, but many years ago, before the coyote had become established in a particular area, folks had other explanations. Everyone in the neighborhood thought the cat was hit by a car and probably made his way into a roadside ditch before taking his last breath. Or they might have blamed the bruiser mutt up the road, and even threatened to sue the mutt's owner if he or she didn't allow them to look in the doghouse for a piece of the missing kitty. Actually, the cat might have been have been grabbed by the jaws of Wily and dragged into a den for a late-night snack. Case closed and no lawsuit filed.

We don't know just how many coyotes there are in North America today. The questionnaire I sent to state and provincial game and fish departments asked if they knew how many coyotes inhabited their state or province. Most were reluctant to take even a wild guess, but I did come up with a few numbers. These population estimates are shown in the accompanying table. Some who would not provide an estimate just said "no" to the question. Some said "unknown," while others summed it up by saying that population surveys are not attempted nor are roadkills monitored.

In Kentucky officials use a comparison of officer reports of furbearing animals that became road fatalities per 10,000 miles driven. For instance, in 1997 officers spotted an average of 2.21 coyotes lying dead per 10,000 miles traveled, but in 1998 they saw 2.50 coyotes. Yes, even a roughly estimated population of coyotes may be derived from counting dead ones lying along roads. However, there's nothing wrong with this. For many years biologists have also counted the dead to determine if populations of foxes, bobcats, raccoons, and other furbearing animals were increasing or decreasing.

Another way to examine populations of coyotes is the hunting harvest. Wildlife agencies do this in states where coyotes are hunted quite often. The state sends a questionnaire to a portion of the hunters to determine the number of coyotes they killed, and in some cases the number of hours they spent in the field. These statistics are compiled annually and compared to determine if coyote numbers are decreasing or increasing. Some states also provide hunters with a sighting questionnaire, which the hunter fills out each time he hunts. It includes a list of animals, and coyotes are never an exception. At the end of the hunting season, the individual returns the sighting questionnaire. In my opinion, this is probably one of the best methods for determining an increase or decrease in numbers of coyotes, particularly when it involves a smaller area such as a particular county. Some hunters are in the field daily and can accurately report this useful information.

*Coyote Populations**

Arizona	150,000—a crude estimate of the spring breeding population
British Columbia	2,000–3,000 in the Lower Mainland; 200 in the city of Vancouver
California	1,000 in the city of Los Angeles
Delaware	Less than 100
Illinois	20,000–30,000
Kentucky	Populations are less dense in the Cumberland Plateau region of eastern Kentucky, more dense in western and central Kentucky
Maine	12,000–16,000
Michigan	150,000–200,000; the maximum potential (carrying capacity) is estimated at 225,000–300,000
Minnesota	Increasing in developed agricultural areas, decreasing in northern forests
Montana	Prior estimates have ranged from a low of 57,000 to an extreme high of 517,000
Nebraska	26,135 were harvested in 1999
New Brunswick	15,000
New Jersey	1,500–2,000
New York	20,000–30,000 (summer population)
Nova Scotia	No formal estimate; varying in the several thousands
Ohio	Population trends according to annual bowhunter surveys (number of coyotes seen per 1,000 hours hunted) suggest that the coyote population is increasing

Coyote Populations (Continued)

Pennsylvania	25,000
Rhode Island	From sightings, roadkills, hunter kills, etc., it's known that they're present in all towns except Black Island
South Carolina	Now in all counties; the population is considered low to moderate but increasing statewide
South Dakota	65,000
Washington	Healthy and abundant
West Virginia	0.5 per square mile and increasing
Wisconsin	20,000

*States and provinces that reported coyote populations or comments on the questionnaire provided by the author. Numbers provided have been roughly estimated, and in some cases, comments are included.

Since coyotes are destined to cause a little trouble wherever they are, some states and provinces can assume their abundance by the number of complaints they receive, and the number of investigations made annually. For instance, Pennsylvania tracks coyote depredation of livestock, pets, and deer as reported by wildlife conservation officers.

Even those officials who did estimate the coyote population found it difficult to provide numbers without adding comments such as "rough estimate," "don't hold me to it," and "numbers of coyotes will have increased considerably by the time this book is in print." As Stanley P. Young noted in 1951:

It is my feeling that the great and constant pressure exerted upon the coyote by man has been a real factor in its spread through the centuries. Even among the human races may be found cases where persecution has encouraged the constant seeking of newer and greener pastures in the attempt at survival. The sum-total of the causes behind this urge to spread on the part of the coyote is a field yet to be thoroughly explored for final answers. It is one of the few animals that has been able to extend its range within historic times.

In their article "Coyote Depredation Control: An Interface Between Biology and Management," published in the *Journal of Range Management,* Frederick F. Knowlton, Eric M. Gese, and Michael M. Jaeger, wildlife research biologists, said that estimates of coyote density range from 0.2 to 2.3 coyotes per square kilometer, with generally increasing densities from the northern to southern United States. They added that available food, especially in winter, is the major factor regulating coyote abundance, mediated by social dominance and territoriality. Food abundance regulates coyote numbers by influencing reproduction, survival, dispersal, space-use patterns, and territory density. During times when snowshoe hare or black-tailed jackrabbit numbers decline (part of the coyote's diet in some areas), studies indicate that coyote populations also decline: Coyotes don't breed as often or have large litters. They also documented that in areas with harsh winters, when carrion is low, coyote pack sizes remain small.

Although the coyote was once limited to the Great Plains of North America, he continues to expand his territory throughout the continent. From Central America to the Arctic, Wily now flourishes. He inhabits every state in the United States and every province in Canada, and no longer walks only the grass-

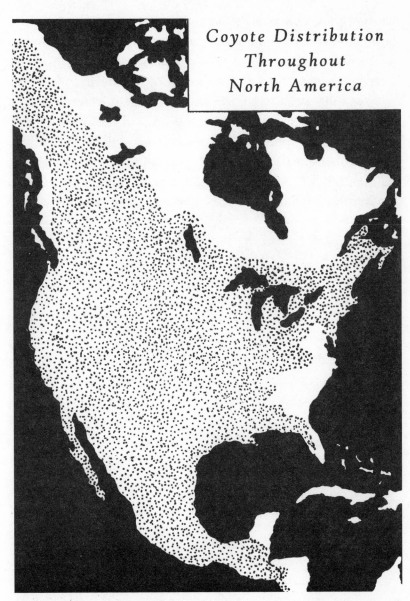

Coyote Distribution
Throughout
North America

The coyote is a native predator of the West; it did not expand into many states and provinces until the turn of the twentieth century.

lands. Today Wily is right at home in deserts, dense forests, farmlands, swamps, and our highest mountains. He has also adjusted quite well to concrete and asphalt, setting up home in many metropolitan areas. Anywhere prey exists, the coyote has, or soon will, become the "top dog." You see, the coyote is a follower, tracking his prey wherever it goes. If the grass appears greener on the other side—and it usually does—he will go there. For instance, when in the grasslands he feeds on sheep; he then follows the herd as it moves into the higher elevation. He is truly a predator of no boundaries.

2

Lifestyles of the Not-So-Famous

QUESTION: *What does a coyote look like?*

ANSWER: *It's brown and fuzzy, and half of his tail is white?*
— Bradley Williams, age 6

I've already discussed how the coyote has expanded his range dramatically, although humans have done their best to oppress him. However, nature has taught us that the survival instinct of many species will become stronger once they are threatened. If habitat exists, they will bounce back and increase their numbers—as if to say, "That ought to teach you a lesson." Centuries of persecution and outright attempts to annihilate the coyote are no big secret, and while these attempts may have reduced his numbers somewhat in a few areas, there has always been a place for Wily to go. He is extremely adaptable. In the pages that follow, you'll see why.

It's a Dog . . . It's a Wolf . . . It's Wily!

The coyote has often been mistaken for other members of the Canidae family, particularly the dog. His closest look-alike is a German shepherd. In areas where the species only recently became established, some folks probably see a coyote but don't take a second look because they think he's a dog. A coyote does compare to a medium-sized one, but he's usually more slender than a dog. Wily also moves with much more grace than your average dog.

Many dogs are larger than even an adult coyote, which typically weighs between 20 and 45 pounds. However, larger coyotes have been reported. Males are usually a few pounds heavier than females. A mature coyote is 42 to 56 inches long, including the 14-inch tail. At the shoulder, the coyote is about 25 inches tall.

Many northern coyotes, probably because of interbreeding with wolves many years ago, will sometimes weigh 50 to 60 pounds. Those in southern states that may have hybridized with red wolves, along with coyotes in the Midwest, usually weigh a few pounds more than the coyotes of the western plains. Desert coyotes seldom weigh more than 22 pounds.

Coydogs—the result of interbreeding between coyotes and domesticated free-roaming dogs—are also larger than the average adult coyote. The rare coydog may weigh more than 60 pounds. Those that exist today carry the genes of those coyotes and dogs that bred many years ago, whenever coyotes first established in a given area. Yet a male dog on the prowl for a glamorous female dog might choose to fight a female coyote, even if she's in heat. Consider, too, that upon seeing a coyote many dogs want to attack. Of course, these dogs usually bite off more than they can chew, even if they're twice the size of their coyote foe. Then there are dogs trained to run and hunt coyotes. Some dogs possess a built-in sense to run them, while others must be taught. Either way, if every male hunting dog thought it best to look for a willing female coyote, then coyote hunting dogs would not exist today.

Wily's color varies from brown to light gray. Some appear blond, while others seem to be black or red when seen at a distance. The coyote's hide is darker in the winter than in the summer. Locality also plays a role in the coloration of the coyote, as does altitude. For instance, those that inhabit the mountains are usually darker than those of the lower elevations. Due to the dark guard hairs on its bushy tail, the tail appears dark with a black tip. Rarely, a coyote with a white-tipped tail is spotted. The coyote's coat often appears shaggy. In early summer Wily's fur is very scruffy and thin, unlike the heavier coat he carries in the winter. The belly, throat, and inside of the ears are almost white.

Many folks have mistaken the coyote for a wolf. Before coyotes were fully established in some areas, people probably saw one and contacted their wildlife agency to report a wolf, even though wolves may have disappeared from the area long ago. An adult wolf is three or more times larger than the coyote. Also different from the coyote is the way a wolf carries his tail. When the coyote walks or runs, his tail becomes almost horizontal—it's close to how the wolf carries the tail but not as high as a dog carries his.

The coyote's head differs considerably from other canids. The snout is elongated, and it has a black nose. The ears are wide, upright, and pointed. Like the wolf, but unlike the dog, Wily has yellow eyes, which allow him to see in the dark much

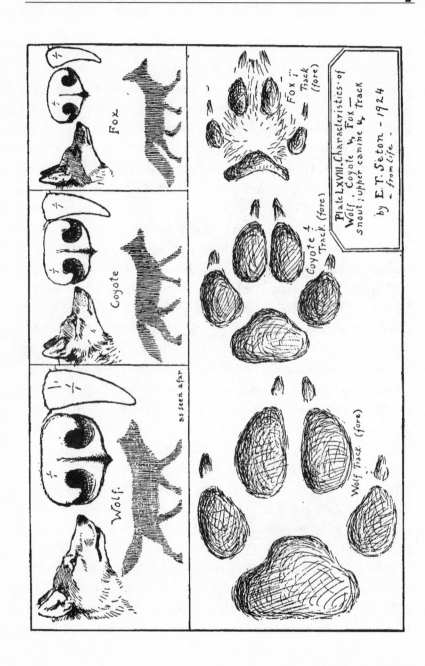

Plate LXVIII. Characteristics of Wolf, Coyote & Fox — snout; upper canine & track

by E.T. Seton – 1924 – from life –

Fox i Track (fore)

Coyote i Track (fore)

Wolf Track (fore)

Fox

Coyote

Wolf

as seen afar

better than we can. Although he has 42 teeth, the 4 remarkably long canine teeth (2 uppers and 2 lowers) are responsible for bringing down his prey.

The coyote's track differs greatly from the track of a dog or wolf. Wily has five toes, as do dogs and wolves, but his track is smaller than that of a wolf's, and usually smaller than a dog's track. Also noticeable is the narrowness of a coyote track. It appears oval and not as round as a dog's track. Tracks are discussed further in chapter 6.

Wily's Habits

Although I have explained how the coyote has moved into new regions during the past century, Wily is not a migrating animal. But some coyotes do have an extremely large home range. Certain habitual requirements, such as food, increase the distance they travel. It has also been noted that females don't roam as far as males. Rearing young probably contributes to this. Nonetheless, once the pups are raised, a coyote might move a considerable distance from the den. For instance, studies done in a few western states show that ear-tagged and radio-collared young coyotes moved 100 miles from where they were born. In Florida a study indicated that the coyote's home range was 1,500 to 12,000 acres.

Coyotes sometimes live solitary lives. Others stay with only their mate. In some instances, packs of coyotes are observed. However, they seldom run in packs the way wolves do. When a pack of coyotes is spotted, it's usually a male, female, and their pups.

The coyote is an excellent hunter, but more important, he is a superb thinker. Many individuals who have studied his hunting habits believe that he's capable of planning an attack. One example of this is Wily's ability to run his prey toward a fence, where the victim's escape will be blocked. He seems to know he might not catch a running jackrabbit on open ground, but the right fence will even up the odds.

Coyotes also work in concert. A lone coyote could possibly take down an adult deer when conditions are favorable, but a couple working together provide more assurance. That's not to say that coyotes often kill deer. On the contrary, deer are not killed and eaten by coyotes as often as most people believe they are. You'll read more about this in the following chapter.

Single coyotes have been observed running an antelope in circles while the mate sits back and watches. When the first coyote becomes exhausted, the second takes over. This continues until the antelope can't take any more.

More proof of coyotes' ability to think has derived from observations of them waiting to catch a mouse while another animal does the work. They sit back and watch as a larger animal hunts, hoping it will send a mouse out of hiding. When the mouse is exposed, the coyote plunges ahead and captures his prey.

Another example of apparent planning by a coyote comes from a Wisconsin man who reported seeing a coyote on three different occasions when he cut grass near a woods. The coyote did not come close, but would sit back and watch. The man believed that the coyote knew that the sounds of the mower would send a rodent out of hiding and heading for the woods where he waited. The coyote probably experienced this enough times to know that the running mower was actually a ringing dinner bell.

The coyote can run up to 40 miles per hour, but he usually relies on speeds of about 25 miles per hour to catch prey. Actually, habitat may influence just how fast a coyote can run. In open country he must often run faster than he does in brushy country.

When a coyote steadily walks or trots in noisy leaves, trained ears can determine that it is indeed a coyote coming. His walk is very deliberate—unlike those of other four-legged animals, such as deer, which take a few steps and stop. I have often heard disturbances in leaf-covered woods and been able to tell that a coyote was about to appear. Sometimes, though, an approaching fox fools me.

A coyote often communicates with his body parts. For example, when Wily becomes aggressive, the hairs of his tail will flare outward and the tail will appear bushier than normal. He moves his ears to show his mood, too. Ear movement is also used to show his rank when he encounters another coyote.

One common trait of coyotes is to follow a trail. They love to walk old roadbeds, deer trails, and other cleared passageways. Feces are often found along such routes, since coyotes instinctually deposit their waste where it can't be missed. Sometimes they defecate on rocks and logs along the trail.

Other than dens, which are prepared for birthing, coyotes spend most of their time during the daylight hours laid up in rock piles, under ledges, in brush, and in logjams. In suburbs and urban areas, they have been discovered in abandoned buildings, under woodpiles, and in drainpipes. Normally, they require minimal cover. Nevertheless, they're excellent diggers and can do the job quickly when they want a den. They will also hang out in a hole dug by another animal. They may need to enlarge the hole, but it beats the heck out of digging a new one.

Wily is primarily a nocturnal predator, although he sometimes ventures out early in the afternoon when favorable

weather occurs. During the winter, especially when snow has
been on the ground for a long time, coyotes are often spotted
moving about in late morning and at midday. In the suburbs
and urban areas coyotes are more susceptible to being spotted
in daylight hours.

The highly adaptable coyote often prefers to do his hunting
in fields, but this depends upon food availability. He also hangs
around woodland fringes and thickets, or wherever some cover
exists. River bottoms have also become a favorite place, as have
backyards and city parks.

Territorial Habits

Within the life of the coyote, pecking orders are usually established. Packs are sometimes spotted, as are solitary animals.
Coyote lifestyles are somewhat affected by these attributes.
Wildlife research biologists Knowlton, Gese, and Jaeger wrote
that coyotes exhibit a dominance hierarchy within packs and a
land-tenure system of exclusive territories; this affects coyote
numbers, because social groups partition the landscape in relation to available habitat and food resources. It was also noted
that social dominance among members of resident packs can
influence access to clumped food resources, such as carcasses.

Older and experienced pack members are more successful
hunters of large prey and small animals. It has also been said
that dominant individuals with access to carcasses are less likely
to disperse.

Acquiring a territory is important to a coyote. A territorial
coyote is much more likely to survive than one that doesn't have
a territory. The territorial coyote will also gain more breeding

Unlike some mammals that have small home ranges, the coyote's territory typically covers several miles.

opportunities, and he's more likely to have access to carcasses in winter than temporary coyotes. But make no mistake: The non-breeding individuals of a pack comprise a significant portion of the coyote population.

If a coyote is in a given territory in summer, you can assume he can also survive there in winter. For this reason coyote densities usually remain the same, changing only when food availability becomes an issue; however, Knowlton, Gese, and Jaeger noted that the size and structure of coyote packs, and hence populations, change seasonally. Births, deaths, and dispersal all have seasonal patterns.

Till Death Do Us Part

Interestingly, 50 percent or more of coyotes die before or during adolescence. Those that do make it to adulthood might enjoy a life span of about 8 to 12 years in the wild. A few captive coyotes have made it even longer, including one at National Zoological Park in Washington, D.C. That coyote lived for 18½ years. Another report indicated that a California livestock owner took a male coyote pup from a den and raised it on his ranch. The tame coyote made it to his 17th birthday. I would suggest, though, you don't consider making a pet out of a coyote. It's illegal in most places to do so, and coyotes don't make good pets.

The coyote has few enemies other than large dogs. As I've mentioned previously, some dogs will go out of their way to attack a coyote. In some areas of the North, wolves will kill a coyote. Other animals are capable of it but seldom try or have any reason to. Humans, although they have declared war on coyotes in some areas, have not posed much of a threat to the coyote's existence. Humankind has already lost the war, but a few battles still occur. Lynx, bears, and eagles occasionally kill coyotes, but these incidents are rare.

However, other than dogs and a few rare battles that humans have won, the usual canine diseases—distemper, hepatitis, parvovirus, tularemia, and rabies—sometimes affect just how long a coyote will live. He also gets ticks, fleas, and mites, which can lead to mange and sometimes death. Some coyotes are affected by heartworms; in California this is considered a major problem. This parasite can be transmitted to dogs by mosquitoes.

When it comes to human-coyote contact, rabies should be a concern, but not necessarily something you should worry yourself about. Most problem coyotes don't carry rabies. Most folks know that rabies is a virus of warm-blooded animals. Once an animal contracts the disease, death usually follows. In rare instances animals have survived rabies. So just how often do coyotes contract the disease? No figures are available, but as are foxes, wolves, skunks, and raccoons, coyotes are susceptible. Less likely candidates among wild animals include rabbits, squirrels, chipmunks, and a few other rodents.

Rabies is transmitted by a bite, scratch, or other contact that allows the saliva of the infected animal to get into the tissue of another. Symptoms of an infected coyote depend upon the type of rabies. Usually the animal shows signs of "dumb rabies": He wanders aimlessly and appears weak and unaware of his surroundings. In other words, if a coyote is walking around carelessly and appears to have no fear of you, he could have rabies. "Furious rabies" occurs when the animal becomes vicious and wants to attack any animal or human. He may even snarl and bite himself. Regardless of which type of rabies an animal has, he may foam at the mouth. If you see a coyote that exhibits any of these symptoms, or one that acts strangely in another manner, contact your local health department.

Despite what I just said about coyotes and rabies, there is little to fear if a coyote stalks you, or even bites you. If a coyote does bite you, chances are the animal doesn't have rabies. With this in mind, I would suggest you don't jump off your roof and end it all before the "going mad" syndrome begins; however, it would be wise to see your physician. Providing you don't wait too long, a vaccine will assure you that even if you contracted rabies, you won't become a statistic. A later chapter discusses the frequency of coyote attacks on humans. For now, I'll get back to rabies and coyotes.

Many states and provinces have never found rabies present in a coyote. Others haven't been so lucky. More than 500 confirmed rabies cases occurred in 18 south Texas counties since 1988, of which 270 were found in coyotes. Fortunately, the state was able to reduce the incidence of canine rabies.

In 1999 the Wildlife Services of the USDA (U.S. Department of Agriculture) provided assistance to the Texas Department of Health to stop the spread of canine rabies in south Texas. A vaccination project, implemented in 1995, was used in an attempt to contain the disease and reduce human exposure. More than 2.5 million rabies vaccine baits were distributed over a 42,000-square-mile area in south Texas, involving 198 aerial bait-drop operations. Results have been astounding. There has been a 96 percent reduction of canine rabies since the first oral vaccine airdrop in south Texas in 1996. Surveillance programs conducted in March 1999 showed that 89 percent of coyotes tested from the area produced evidence of immune response to the vaccine. In fact, reported canine rabies cases in south Texas have declined from 166 in 1994 to 7 in 1998 and 8 from mid-March through November 1999. Similar success was also observed in the gray fox, despite a growing population of that species.

Well-Tuned Senses

All animals, including humans, are gifted with senses. However, the varying acuity of these senses affects our daily lives. Human senses don't compare to the well-tuned senses of some animals, including the coyote. It's also interesting to note how each animal seems to possess one sense that's more acute than the others. A bear has poor eyesight and pretty good hearing, but relies primarily on his sense of smell for everyday survival. The antelope and wild turkey have excellent eyesight, which is responsible for their ability to escape predators more often than not.

As for Wily, he could be the most gifted of all animals. His sense of smell is probably his keenest, but his sight and hearing are nearly as acute. All three of these senses play a major role in his life. Scenting prey allows him to locate and get close to the victim before he launches an attack. He also has the ability to spot movement from a long distance in dense country. In addition, he can home in on sounds that we would probably never hear. Overall, I would say that his sense of hearing ranks second.

Coyotes, like most other mammals, have scent glands. You've probably seen dogs the first time two of them meet. Even if they want to tear into each other, they usually sniff the back end of their opponent first. Then the fight will begin—or they'll decide to play or do something else that dogs do. Coyotes' scent glands are also located on the base of their tail (trappers often use this scent to attract coyotes), and they will scent each other just as dogs will. They will also urinate on something and mark their territory, similar to the way dogs urinate on your tire or favorite shrub.

The coyote's physical senses play vital roles in his survival, but many believe it's another sense that contributes the most. Wily seems to have an uncanny way of knowing what's about to happen. This discrete ability, known as ESP (extra-sensory perception), has become the real savior of the coyote's life.

Music to Our Ears

The howling of a coyote is something you don't forget. When you hear his serenade for the first time, you're in awe. It's truly a gift from the wild, and though the eerie howling might cause your nerves to unravel briefly, the song soon becomes peaceful and relaxing. Add to the music of one howling coyote the harmony of two or more howling alongside, and you will feel blessed.

Some folks don't know a coyote is within miles until he howls. Others don't know it even after they hear the howl. When a coyote howls, he usually begins with a couple of short yips. The yips are followed by a long, high-pitched squall, and sometimes a couple more yips. He prefers to do his howling from open areas where the sound will carry. Some folks also believe that a howling coyote is able to pass along useful information to other coyotes, aside from announcing his precise location.

Just how often a coyote will howl depends upon several factors. Some coyotes howl frequently; others seldom do so. Some

Western coyotes were nicknamed "song dogs" for good reason.

coyotes are provoked into howling by other coyotes. In many urban areas folks have noted coyotes howling to sirens and other high-frequency sounds. A coyote might howl anytime, but many wait for a cold, still winter evening at dusk. Nevertheless, they also howl during the early-morning hours and during the night. A glimmering moon need not be present. It has also been determined that coyotes howl more during autumn and winter than they do in spring and summer.

So does Wily also bark like a dog? You bet he does. However, this occurs less frequently than howling. Coyotes seldom bark unless provoked. For instance, a couple of years ago while bear hunting in northern Idaho, my wife, Vikki, and I followed along an old trail toward our vehicle. Dusk was upon us and the mountainside was tranquil. As we rounded a corner in the darkness, we surprised a coyote less than 20 yards away. He bolted instantly and ran away, but not before he barked twice.

Many folks who have surprised a coyote have also heard him bark. However, the bark should not be confused with Wily's typical *yip-yap*. Coyote yips have often been mistaken for an animal in distress, but coyotes yip almost as often as they howl. A coyote in distress sounds like any injured dog. In fact, I would not be able to tell the difference between the sounds of a distressed dog and of an injured coyote unless I was an eyewitness (I have been on more than one occasion) to the animal in trouble.

It was the western coyote that was named "song dog," and for good reason. However, today the song dog is heard in the East as well, and in some urban areas. Wily loves to sing regardless of where he resides, probably because he loves to be heard. So what should you do when you hear the song of the coyote nearby? Take a deep breath and sigh, for you have heard one of nature's foremost tunes.

Making and Raising Baby Wilys

Many wildlife experts say that coyotes are monogamous animals. This word is often misrepresented, however, because the word *monogamy* has three definitions. The first is the act of being married to only one person. The second is the act of marrying only once in a lifetime. The third, a zoological term, simply means, "having only one mate." Since coyotes don't get married, we should resort to the third definition. Some experts claim, though, that a mating pair of coyotes will remain together for years, but may not stay together forever even if both remain alive. With this in mind, we can say that coyotes are *primarily* monogamous.

A female that breeds for the first time might attract several males long before she actually mates. The males will follow her everywhere and wait for her to choose the one she likes best. She selects her mate sometimes a month or more before the breeding begins.

Coyotes breed once a year, usually in February or March—although they may breed as early as January in southern states. Research indicates that a variation of two months exists from northern areas to southern locales. Both males and females reach sexual maturity within a year, usually about 10 months after being born. Occasionally, a coyote will not mate until near two years of age.

When the breeding is about to begin, an older pair that has bred before may select a den that they used previously for giving birth and raising the young. Alternatively, they may reconstruct another burrowing animal's den or sometimes they'll dig a new one. Preferred den locations include holes in steep banks, rock piles, hollow logs, and holes in the ground under brush piles. Studies have indicated that most coyote dens are located on sunny, southern slopes. When a den is dug, a wide mound of dirt can be seen at the base of the den opening or openings (some dens have more than one entrance hole). When the pair goes in and out, they walk to the sides of the mound instead of over the top. A den may be 5 feet deep, though even 20 feet is not out of the question. Still, the coyote is smart enough to know that one den may not do the trick. To increase the chance of the young surviving should danger threaten, the pair may dig two or more dens so that they can move at a moment's notice. Coyotes may also use the second den when cleanliness or fleas become an issue. Although the female does a good job of removing feces and other undesirable debris in the den, a large litter may lead to more than she can handle.

The gestation period for a pregnant coyote is about 60 days. The springtime litter averages from five to eight, but may be larger when food is abundant. Litters of 10 and more have been discovered; in Modoc County, California, officials discovered a litter of 14 pups. It has also been noted that the first litter of a juvenile female may average fewer pups than the litters of mature females.

Coyote pups, like other members of the dog family, are born blind and helpless. They will stay in the den for about two weeks, until just after their eyes open. When they come out of the den the first few times, they don't travel far, usually coming

When they reach six to eight weeks old, coyotes starting leaving the den for sunshine, play, and hunting lessons.

out only to play and gather up sunshine. The pups are weaned after six to eight weeks. During this time, both parents care for the young. The male and female often regurgitate food for the pups as they introduce them to foods other than milk. This same practice occurs in the wild dogs of Africa.

As the pups get older, the male often brings prey to the female and the youngsters. By the time the pups are six to nine months old, they will disperse. A few may stay nearby, while others seek new territory up to 50 miles away or more. The greater the amount of food available in a given area, the closer the pups will stay to their den. They may even stay with the parents to form a pack.

Pup mortality is often high. Distemper and roundworms take their toll. Other coyotes also kill some pups as they venture into new territory. However, when the pups leave their parents, they leave as proficient hunters. For several weeks they have been trained to kill. Most of the youngsters will have little trouble killing their prey when they find it, but if food is scarce, they will travel as far as necessary to locate it.

Satisfying Hunger Pains

The real question is whether we should classify the coyote as a carnivore or omnivore. Some wildlife specialists say he is a carnivore, others an omnivore. Just so you know the difference: Carnivorous animals are predators that eat the flesh of other animals; omnivores may eat flesh, fruit, and vegetation. One thing we do know is that Wily is a skilled predator that consistently practices carnivorous tactics.

Because of the coyote's ability to kill, he has become a nuisance to many folks. He must satisfy his hunger pains, even if it means stealing his prey from humans. Since this book is about solving coyote problems, I have devoted the next two chapters to those foods that made this book possible. For now, I'll briefly discuss Wily's natural, wild foods that don't affect you and me directly.

Most of what we know about coyote foods comes from the study of their feces and sometimes stomach contents. Of course, primary foods may vary from coyote to coyote, simply because of the location where the study occurred, the abundance of a certain food, and the time of year when the study was conducted. Here's a rundown of the coyote's natural menu:

Forty Natural and Wild Coyote Foods*

Beetles	Eggs (all kinds)	Ducks	Geese
Chipmunks	Raccoons	Deer	Antelope
Grasshoppers	Locusts	Berries	Beechnuts
Marmots	Wild turkeys	Fish	Crabs
Apples	Rats	Prairie dogs	Woodchucks
Mice	Voles	Rabbits	Locusts
Moose	Carrion	Foxes	Cats
Pheasants	Songbirds	Elk	Beavers
Snakes	Lizards	Gophers	Worms
Squirrels	Grouse	Quail	Porcupines

*Excludes various grasses and some vegetation.

Take note that not every coyote has access to each of the foods mentioned in the table. Some foods are available only in certain regions during certain seasons. Also, note that it would be impossible for me to list every thing that has been digested by a coyote in the last 100 years. But make no mistake—Wily is not very hard to please when it comes to eating, feeding on carcasses as well as preying upon live mammals. It's probably not the taste of one thing or another that attracts him; instead, hunger pains are dependent upon the availability of a certain food. Nevertheless, aside from coyotes located near people, a coyote's feeding habits vary greatly, depending on several factors.

Wildlife research biologists Eric M. Gese, Robert L. Ruff, and Robert L. Crabtree examined the influence of certain factors in the Lamar Valley of Yellowstone National Park, Wyoming, to determine how they affect the coyote's feeding habits. The biologists considered age, sex, and social status, as well as snow depth, snowpack hardness, temperature, habitat, and available ungulate (hooved mammals) carcasses from January 1991 to June 1993. They observed 54 coyotes during the period, of which 49 were residents from five packs, while the balance were considered temporary visitors. Their studies indicated that coyotes decreased traveling and hunting and increased resting and feeding on carcasses as snow depth and available carcasses increased. The age and social status of the coyotes also influenced their activities. When the snow was deep and a number of carcasses existed, pups fed less on carcasses and hunted small mammals more than alpha (pack leaders) and beta (seconds in command) coyotes. It was determined that the pups were probably restricted by older pack mammals from feeding on carcasses. For this reason, pups practiced a different foraging strategy and fed on small mammals more often.

When it comes down to killing, the coyote has no qualms about being a bad sport and stalking the easiest prey to catch. It's not too hard sneaking up on a blueberry bush, apple, or roadkill. When it comes to killing and eating an animal with functioning senses, however, Wily prefers to go with the one that's easiest to catch.

3

Coyotes and Game Animals

QUESTION: *What do coyotes like to eat?*

ANSWER: *I think they like to eat bears.*
        —Robbie Williams, age 8

F or many years wildlife specialists have been concerned about coyote predation of game animals. Do coyotes significantly reduce game populations, and if so, how much? Wildlife experts aren't the only ones concerned, however. Hunters and wildlife viewers also demand answers and are sometimes quick to blame coyotes when they see fewer game animals. After all, state and provincial wildlife departments manage game populations in various ways, including regulating the number of animals to be killed, and determining hunting season dates. But these specialists can't tell Wily how many game animals he should feast upon.

The effects of coyote predation on game animals are sometimes anyone's guess. Studies indicate both positive and negative views about controlling coyotes to increase game populations. Perhaps we should consider one important fact: Game populations have always been and always will be subject to predation.

Studies indicate frequent findings of game animals in coyote scat, particularly in wilderness areas where fewer humans reside. In an article prepared by G. R. Parker, "The Seasonal Diet of Coyotes in Northern New Brunswick," it was determined that deer and snowshoe hares are a large portion of the coyote's diet.

Parker's study involved the collection of coyote scats in an extreme northern region of New Brunswick. The summers in the area are normally hot with moderate rainfall, while low temperatures and considerable snow accumulation characterize the winters.

Field personnel collected scats on logging roads from May through November 1983, and from January through March 1984, along coyote trails. Each scat collected was stored in a paper bag and kept frozen. The analyses of them identified bone, teeth, nail fragments, and feathers.

Analyses of 383 coyote scats showed that snowshoe hare and white-tailed deer were the most frequently consumed food items throughout the year. Vegetation was commonly consumed, even in winter if grasses and sedges were exposed along stream edges. In late summer many scats contained raspberry seeds. Small mammals and songbirds were occasionally consumed throughout the year, while insects comprised trace components of the diet only during the snow-free period. Another important component during spring and early summer was the groundhog.

Parker determined that snowshoe hare remained the major component of the diet during all seasons, while white-tailed deer consumption was greatest in the winter and least during midsummer. There was a high incidence of deer in the May sample, which is believed to have resulted from the feeding on carcasses recently exposed by the receding snow cover; it didn't represent additional direct mortality. Similarly, a high occurrence of deer in January appeared to be a result from scavenging on carcasses left from the hunting season.

Snowshoe hare comprised 82 percent of the material in scats containing that food item. Groundhog was second at 70 percent, while deer was third at 66 percent. Songbirds, small mammals, and insects were 20 percent or less.

In many areas where groundhogs were once plentiful, folks claim to have seen a reduction in the animals shortly after coyotes arrived on the scene. Destruction of habitat may also have a bearing on the number of groundhogs in a given area, but I will attest to coyotes contributing to their reduction. I have seen a major decline of woodchucks in southern Indiana, and have observed coyotes stalking and attacking them.

According to Parker, this study emphasized the importance of snowshoe hare in the annual diet of coyotes in northern New Brunswick. He claimed that although the groundhog was of seasonal importance, this food source would be unavailable for much of the year. The second most important prey species was the white-tailed deer, which contributed to the diet of coyotes year round. Parker added that a low incidence of deer in the June-through-August samples suggests that predation upon fawns in summer was not of major significance, however. This finding is in contrast to results of other studies in the United States, such as some that have been done in Wisconsin, Texas, Oregon, and Colorado.

Although coyotes feed upon white-tailed deer, many of them are only scavenged after a severe winter kills them.

Considerable evidence shows that deer is often found in scats, particularly in northern and forested portions of the coyote's range. The authors of these studies attribute this to carrion feeding and seldom consider direct predation, explained Parker.

We must also wonder just how often a coyote is successful when attempting to kill a big game animal. An article by Eric M. Gese and Scott Grothe, "Analysis of Coyote Predation on Deer and Elk During Winter in Yellowstone National Park, Wyoming," discussed observations of nine predation attempts by coyote on deer and elk from 1991 to 1993. Gese and Grothe noted that five of the attempts were successful. The details of those predation attempts are as follows:

1. November 1991: A beta female coyote was bedded 50 yards from a white-tailed deer standing in a meadow where some snow was present. Minutes later the coyote stood and rushed twice at the deer, but the deer avoided the coyote. Minutes later the deer charged the coyote. The coyote proceeded to leave and bed down a short distance away. As the deer moved through a creek and onto a gravel bar, another coyote arrived and joined with the other coyote. The two predators began approaching the deer, but the deer began stomping its front hooves at the coyotes. The coyotes retreated and darkness soon arrived. The following day no evidence was found to indicate there were any more attempts by the two coyotes to kill the deer.

2. December 1991: An alpha pair and two beta males of the Norris coyote pack were observed chasing an adult cow elk with a calf through a snow-covered meadow. The pursuit lasted 31 seconds but the elk were able to elude the four coyotes, reaching the Lamar River.

3. January 1993: An alpha male and beta male coyote of the Druid pack chased a lone adult cow elk through a snow-covered grassland area. Two minutes after the chase began, both coyotes clasped their jaws onto the elk's rump. The elk ran into deep snow at the base of a gully and fell. Other coyotes soon joined the first two in the attack. They fed on the live elk, which frequently struggled to stand, but the elk could not get up. The two-year-old elk was assumed dead approximately 25 minutes after the attack began.

4. January 1993: A lone adult cow elk was bedded in a
    snow-covered meadow. The elk had been in the same
    area for 12 days. A male and female coyote that had also
    been bedded in the meadow proceeded toward the elk.
    The male coyote grabbed the elk by the right rear leg
    and hung on as the elk kicked. The female coyote at-
    tempted to attack the abdomen of the elk, but she hesi-
    tated and retreated from the elk's thrashing hooves. Af-
    ter dragging the male coyote, the elk finally collapsed.
    The male coyote released his grip, and the elk got back
    to its feet. However, it didn't last long. The male coyote
    attached himself again and the elk went down. The fe-
    male also grabbed hold of a hind leg as the elk at-
    tempted to get up and run away. The elk was assumed
    dead about 1¼ hours after the attack started. An exami-
    nation of the carcass indicated the elk was approxi-
    mately 15 years old.

5. February 1993: A beta male coyote bedded in a
    meadow not far from a lone calf elk standing in a
    creek. An alpha pair of coyotes bedded in the same
    vicinity. When the elk stepped onto the bank to feed,
    it was noticed she had tufts of hair missing, and fa-
    vored one leg as it dragged through snow. When the
    elk bedded, a coyote would occasionally approach.
    The elk would stand and face the approaching coyote.
    Darkness soon arrived without incident. However,
    the following morning, blood was found in the beds
    where the elk had lain, indicating it was wounded, but
    had escaped being killed.

6. February 1993: An alpha pair of coyotes walking
    through snow-covered sage chased and attacked a calf
    elk below a cliff. After a few minutes, the elk was ob-
    served lying in a creek, while the coyotes watched from
    the bank. The elk had a large, bleeding wound on the
    right rump. The muzzle and chest of the male coyote
    were also covered with blood. Both coyotes bedded
    near the creek, waited, and watched. Darkness soon
    came, but observers at midnight say the elk was still
    alive. The following morning the coyotes were seen
    feeding on the dead elk.

7. March 1993: A lone calf elk was bedded in a snow-
    covered meadow for several hours. As three coyotes
    of the Druid pack approached, the elk stood up. One
    minute later the three coyotes rushed the elk and
    knocked it to the ground. As the coyotes fed on the
    rump of the elk, it tried to get up on five occasions.
    Eventually, a coyote went to the neck, pulled the elk's
    neck to the ground, and held it. The elk vocalized
    during the entire attack. The elk was dead 13 minutes
    after the attack started.

8. March 1993: After a calf elk climbed a snow-covered
    slope, an alpha pair of coyotes rushed in. The male coy-
    ote bit at the elk's rear hamstring. The elk kicked, spun,
    and lifted the coyote off the ground as it struggled to
    get away in deep snow. Meanwhile, the female coyote
    followed closely. The male coyote had released its hold
    when the calf fell, but was able to grab it again. The pair
    attacked the elk three times from the rear and side. As

the elk stood, the male jumped and bit into the elk's neck. The elk appeared dead about 17 minutes after the attack first began.

9. March 1993: An alpha pair of coyotes chased a calf elk along a snow-covered slope. The alpha male led the attack. The elk was able to get out of the snow and onto snow-free ground before the male could attack. The elk ran as the male lunged, and it kicked and struck the male in the left side and shoulder. Meanwhile, the male stopped its attack and appeared stunned. The female stayed beside the male coyote. A short time later the elk joined another herd of elk. Later, two adult cow elk charged the alpha pair, chasing them away. The calf elk appeared to be uninjured.

Another study done by Gary Brundige, a graduate student at the State University of New York College of Environmental Science and Forestry at Syracuse, New York, estimated that white-tailed deer made up in excess of 80 percent of the coyote's diet during winter in the Adirondack Mountains. This evaluation followed the examination of more than 1,000 coyote scats.

A study in Maine, which involved the examination of stomachs from autumn- and early-winter-killed coyotes, showed deer were found in 15.9 percent of the samples. The study concluded, though, that there was no evidence that deer were a staple food.

As for Parker's study, it can be summarized like this: In a wilderness area snowshoe hare was the most important food item in all seasons. White-tailed deer was fed upon in winter and early spring but was of minor importance in summer. Groundhog was an important food in May and June, and rasp-berries in mid to late summer.

From 1972 to 1980 research was conducted on the effects of coyote control on white-tailed deer populations at the Welder Wildlife Refuge in south Texas. To keep coyotes away from deer, specialists constructed a mesh, net-wire fence 6 feet above the ground, and a 12-inch extension under the ground around a 1,000-acre pasture. On top of the fence an electrically charged wire was used to discourage coyotes from climbing. Several methods were used to remove coyotes from the enclosure. After the study concluded, it was determined that white-tailed fawn survival was 30 percent higher in the enclosure than on the rest of the refuge.

Enclosing deer herds to keep them away from coyotes isn't the answer, however. The deer herd in the study did increase for five years, but declined sharply when its food supply dwindled and parasites increased. The enclosed deer also subsisted on a crude, low-protein diet. Eventually, the health of the enclosed deer herd improved as the food supply returned to a normal level.

Of those states and provinces that responded to my questionnaire, several answered the question asking which game animals suffer most from coyote attacks. Keep in mind, however, that not all of these answers come from studies conducted on coyote feces and stomach contents. In many cases, the specialist who answered the question simply gave an opinion. Of those states that responded to the questionnaire, some answered this question by saying "unknown."

Game Animals That Suffer Most from Coyote Attacks*

State or Province	Game Animals Preyed Upon Most Often
Alaska	Probably only Dall sheep lambs
Arizona	Cottontail rabbits
California	Jackrabbits
Florida	Probably cottontail rabbits; coyotes are not known to have much impact on deer
Georgia	Rabbits, but in general coyotes are not a limiting factor for any game species
Kansas	Antelope populations are probably regulated by coyotes; however, coyotes eat more rabbits than deer or antelope
Kentucky	Cottontail rabbits
Maine	White-tailed deer
Michigan	Rabbits and hares
Montana	Mule deer; when small mammals (mice and voles) are at low population levels, coyotes seem to switch to deer
Nebraska	Probably deer, but deer numbers are high and losses due to coyotes are insignificant
New Brunswick	Deer, cottontail rabbits, and snowshoe hares
Nova Scotia	Deer and snowshoe hares
Ohio	Both red and gray foxes probably suffer most; public perception is that deer occasionally suffer from coyote attacks, but this is unfounded
Oklahoma	Deer fawn mortality is high in some areas of the state due to coyotes, but animals that are affected most are rabbits, quail, and other small game species

Game Animals That Suffer Most (Continued)

State or Province	Game Animals Preyed Upon Most Often
Oregon	Coyotes prey upon all Oregon game mammals in their territories
Pennsylvania	Snowshoe hares, cottontail rabbits, squirrels, turkeys, and grouse are taken in the greatest numbers; however, the only predation reports received from the public involve deer
South Carolina	Probably cottontail rabbits
South Dakota	Variable from year to year
Utah	Antelope and deer
West Virginia	White-tailed fawn
Wisconsin	Rabbits and squirrels are preyed upon commonly—although this is not a concern; prey populations are stable to increasing.

*As reported by various states and provinces.

Coyotes also enjoy eating various species of ducks and geese, particularly those that become residents near your lake or pond. This is true of waterfowl in both rural and urban areas. Coyotes also prey upon migrating waterfowl, but often rely upon nesting birds or those that set up permanent homes in rural areas once they realize these birds are easy prey. However, coyotes may not prey upon waterfowl as often as other predators, such as the red fox.

Coyotes will sometimes kill red and gray foxes and bobcats. Feeding upon foxes and bobcats occurs less often, however. Coyotes seem to possess a special hatred for some predators smaller than them and may kill them just for sport, or at least chase them for sport.

We can't assume that Wily considers another predator equal, or that he sees it as competition, but coyote killings of foxes and bobcats have been observed on many occasions. Many trappers, upon their arrival to check a trap, attest to coyotes tearing into or feeding on foxes and bobcats caught there. Hunters have also enjoyed success using fox calls to attract coyotes. Coyotes have also been seen running bobcats up a tree. Nevertheless, a coyote could get more than he could handle when attacking a bobcat—these are fierce cats, to say the least. The same principle applies to domestic dogs and cats. Spike the dog will chase Fancy the kitty, even though Fancy is capable of making Spike wish he'd never left the doghouse that day.

Wild turkeys are also part of the coyote's diet. However, since the boom in wild turkey populations came only during the past three decades, wildlife experts haven't really determined just how often coyotes kill and eat wild turkeys, and if they're having any effect on the growth of turkey populations.

Only a few months before preparing this chapter, I stopped my truck to watch a hen turkey as she walked casually across a narrow field. Moments later I spotted another animal standing perfectly still in the field, no more that 40 yards from the turkey. I assumed the animal standing motionless was a coyote, and my binoculars verified this a few seconds later. Then I witnessed the astounding hunting ability of the coyote. There was no telling how long he had been in the field, but he knew it was best to remain stationary and wait for the hen to make a mistake. She was coming closer to him; soon she would be within snatching distance. He would need to charge at her only if he could catch her before she went airborne.

It was not my intention to spoil the predator's hunt, but when I opened the door to lean over the hood of my truck for a better view, the turkey spotted me, turned, and walked away from the coyote, into the safety of the woods. Meanwhile, the coyote hadn't noticed my presence. When the turkey left, he sat down on his haunches as if to say, "Oh well, nothing ventured, nothing gained." Yet, it's my opinion that the coyote would have failed even if I hadn't intervened. He was standing in the open with nothing but air between him and the hen.

Although I've attempted to determine just how many turkeys wind up on the coyote's dinner table, there were little or no data available to substantiate that coyotes do indeed prey upon turkeys. Oh yes, examined scat and stomach content indicate that coyotes have fed upon game birds. Nevertheless, in looking through several coyote books found on my outdoor bookshelf and scanning several research papers by biologists, I found no discussions of coyotes feeding upon wild turkeys. Perhaps this is because the turkey is still the "new kid on the block" in some areas.

Turkey hunters probably provide the most convincing proof that coyotes have discovered the taste of wild turkey, have enjoyed it immensely, and are making it a point to come back for seconds. The real question is just how often wild turkeys are attacked and killed by coyotes.

Turkey hunters, when calling to turkeys during the hunting season, often attract coyotes. Coyotes have also been observed attacking turkey decoys. A camouflaged hunter and a turkey decoy, though, are not the real thing. Thus, if a coyote sneaks up on a decoy or a turkey call, he's usually observed by the hunter. A turkey hunter may then assume that the predator makes a meal out of a wild turkey more often than not, but those who know the wild turkey also understand that this bird's eyesight is second to nothing. Their eyes sit neatly on the sides of their head, giving them extensive peripheral vision. Naturally, the decoy that the coyote sneaks up on cannot see.

When a coyote does kill a wild turkey, it's probably a spring gobbler more often than it's a hen. When the spring mating season nears, gobblers begin strutting. In the process their tail feathers are expanded. This blocks their vision from the backside, allowing a predator to close in for the kill.

David Hale of Knight & Hale Game Calls has shot a number of spring gobblers that had several missing tail feathers. He says this is one sign that a predator attempted to attack the bird. However, he believes there's far more predation on turkeys from bobcats in some areas, and far more damage to turkey populations due to raccoons raiding turkey nests. Still, this doesn't necessarily mean that coyotes aren't attracted to turkey talk and turkey decoys.

As I mentioned, wild turkeys rely primarily on their eyes for survival. We also know their numbers continue to increase despite the expansion of coyotes in North America. Thus, I believe it safe to say that coyotes are not a threat to the survival of wild turkeys.

A major study of coyote stomachs began in the 1930s. I say "major" because it involved the analysis of 14,289 coyote stomachs from 17 states during all seasons of the year, and took 10 years to complete. The largest number of stomachs examined came from Washington (1,186). Fewer than 100 stomachs were examined from Nebraska (70), South Dakota (97), Michigan (88), Missouri (6), and Wisconsin (7). More than 1,000 stomachs were also collected from Colorado and New Mexico. In Arizona, California, Idaho, Montana, Nevada, Oregon, Texas, Utah, and Wyoming, between 145 and 918 stomachs were examined. Not all of the stomachs collected provided data. Some were empty, while others contained only debris. Of all the stomachs collected, 8,339 were analyzed.

With the exception of midwinter, rabbit was found most often in the coyote's diet throughout the year. Rabbit was present in 43 percent of the stomachs in each of the 17 states. Another group of rodents was third in the coyote's diet, which includes squirrels, marmots, and groundhogs. As for big game animals, antelope, bear, bighorn sheep, bison, deer, and elk totaled 3.58 percent of the coyote's diet. Eighty percent consisted of rodents, rabbits, carrion, insects, vegetable matter, and other animals. Big game animals were included in the remaining 20 percent, along with other animals and birds. Game birds made up 1 percent of the diet, as did nongame birds.

Squirrels, hares, rabbits, raccoons, and a variety of game birds are often included in the coyote's diet. However, most specialists don't feel the population of small game animals is severely affected by predation. When coyotes feed upon some big game animals, such as antelope, there are other arguments to consider.

It's no big secret that coyotes sometimes feed upon antelope in western states and provinces. Just how many pronghorns are killed remains a question. In studies of coyote scats in the West, antelope was commonly found. Many folks blame decreases in antelope herds on predation, but this is only sometimes the cause. Coyotes have lived alongside pronghorns for hundreds

Do coyotes significantly reduce pronghorn herds? Researchers remain skeptical.

of years, and they haven't eradicated the antelope. They may have some impact on an antelope population, but when a herd decreases substantially in a certain area, loss of habitat, a stretch of severe winters, or overgrazing of the habitat by livestock is often the cause.

When it comes to coyotes and pronghorns, there are two sides to the story. Everybody seems to have an opinion: some against Wily, some for. Are coyotes responsible when an antelope population decreases? Should they be killed to make certain the herd grows? The argument goes on.

In Oregon, on the Hart Mountain Antelope Refuge, there was an increase of about 500 antelope fawns in one year, despite the absence of a coyote control program. Animal activists rejoiced in the news, but refuge officials are skeptical, claiming that the pronghorn population fluctuates up and down consistently, and is still nowhere near a population high that occurred in the early 1990s. Wildlife officials still blame Wily for the overall decline. The refuge wants to use predator control, and the activists do not. The battle there continues.

Not long ago I put the binoculars on a coyote as he came over a hill in the prairies of central Montana. I was sitting in a pile of hay bales, was hidden completely, and had an excellent view. At the bottom of the hill about 50 antelope lay bedded in the sagebrush. I noticed that the coyote did not attempt to sneak into the herd of pronghorns. Instead, he walked casually into the middle of the group and gracefully moved around without showing any sign of wanting to prey upon them. I expected the antelope to put it into high gear when the coyote approached, but to my surprise each stayed put and stared a hole through the predator. The coyote meandered within 30 to 40 yards of several pronghorns, but each time the antelope would stand up, face into him, and glare. However, each pronghorn seemed to sense he would not attack.

Coyotes probably kill antelope fawns much more often than adults, but even then, it's those fawns younger than a couple of weeks old that are usually caught. It was September when I watched the coyote waltz through the antelope herd, and although there were several fawns in the herd, they were three months old and wouldn't have been easy catches. Most fawns can outrun a coyote at four or five days old. I'm sure the coyote knew this, too. I also wondered if the coyote was looking for a crippled pronghorn. Had he discovered such a candidate, he probably would have attacked.

But make no mistake: Coyotes don't routinely feed only upon lame or sick antelope, or other weak game animals, livestock, or pets for that matter. The belief that predators kill only the injured or ill is a misconception. It's nature's rule that the unhealthy will be eliminated one way or another: sometimes by the elements and sometimes by predators. And it's true that a coyote may find it easier to prey upon a sick or injured animal than one that's healthy. Nevertheless, if Wily had to prey upon only the weak to survive, this book wouldn't be necessary.

Of course there are some wildlife experts who believe that a reduction in predators could increase antelope herds. However, as always we must consider the facts. Charles L. Cadieux, a free-lance writer-photographer and antelope expert who spent more than 30 years working with state and U.S. wildlife agencies studying pronghorns and informing the public about wildlife management, made the following observations in *Pronghorn, North America's Unique Antelope:*

1. Coyotes do kill newborn antelope, and have been shown to be the limiting factor on some antelope herds.
2. Predators have preyed on pronghorns for millennia, and they were not a limiting factor in the centuries prior to man's usurpation of pronghorn range for his own purposes.
3. Upon rare occasions, coyotes have been known to kill healthy adult pronghorns. The number of times this happens is statistically insignificant, according to most authorities.
4. Factors that reduce the pronghorn's mobility increase the damaging effects of predation; for example, woven-wire fences may increase the pronghorn's vulnerability to mortality caused by coyotes.

5. Pronghorn numbers showed a significant i
    the introduction of Compound 1080, the m   ive
    coyote-killing agent ever developed. Some ma, argue
    that this is a case of *"Post hoc, ergo propter hoc"* reasoning,
    but the timing can hardly be coincidental, and the re-
    sults are inarguably evident.

Although a single coyote usually preys upon small game animals, it seldom kills large adult game animals. For the most
part, it takes two and often more coyotes to bring down a large
game animal, such as a deer or antelope. Snow is another factor. The deeper the snow and the longer it's on the ground,
the better the chance that coyotes will bring down a large
game animal.

The real question lies in how much we value game animals
and how much should be spent protecting them from predation, when predation becomes a factor. All wildlife has substantial value. Consider the fees collected for hunting licenses,
habitat protection, and restoration stamps, as well as the intan-
gible value many receive from viewing and photographing
wildlife. According to M. J. Bodenchuk, J. R. Mason, and W. C.
Pitt, in *Economics of Wildlife Damage,* soon to be published by the
Colorado State University Press, threatened and endangered
species have been judged "incalculable." They added that estimates of minimum value can be calculated from the funds ex-
pended for restoration. These include the costs of captive
breeding projects, refuge expenditures for the protection of the
species, and funds spent by the public on mitigation projects.
Bodenchuk, Mason, and Pitt also concluded that managing coyote populations will improve fawn survival:

Both mule deer and pronghorn fawn survival can be increased by management actions that decrease predation by coyotes (e.g., Hailey 1979, Knowlton 1976). For the latter, predation of unprotected fawns can approach 90 percent, although factors such as alternative prey, age structure of the coyote population and synchrony of fawning all play a factor (Dunbar et al. 1999, Byers 1997).

When predation management programs are implemented, pronghorn fawn survival and the recruitment of young individuals into the adult population increase dramatically. Smith et al. (1986) noted that predation management could result in 100 percent annual increases in population size. In general, management activities that remove coyotes after breeding territories are established but prior to fawning, can double fawning success.

Similarly, mule deer fawn survival can be increased when coyote populations are seasonally suppressed in fawning habitat.

As for direct costs and benefits of coyote removal, the biologists addressed several big-game management areas in Utah. Here are their findings.

- *Henry Mountains mule deer:* After aerial gunning and ground removal of coyotes, the cumulative cost of fawn protection during 1997 and 1998 was $15,841. However, the herd size increased by 600 animals. The civil value assigned to mule deer is $300. Accordingly, the net benefit for two years work totaled $180,000.

- **Bookcliffs mule deer:** After intensive aerial hunting of coyotes on fawning grounds, and a cost of $11,100, the herd size increased by 667 animals. The net benefit was $200,100.

- **Pahvant mule deer:** Three years of deer fawn protection using coyote removals cost $27,480, but resulted in an increase of 2,073 fawns worth $621,900.

- **Pronghorn:** Protection has been extensively evaluated (much more than mule deer) and is almost always considered to be cost beneficial. For example, Smith et al. (1986) evaluated the benefit cost of predation management using the cost of pronghorn permits plus estimated hunter expenditures. A management schedule that involved the removal of territorial coyotes every year yielded the greatest return.

Clearly, the predation management program to protect wildlife is probably worth the expense. In 1998 Wildlife Services programs in the Western Region spent $2,936,068 (federal and cooperative combined) on this activity. However, the benefits of Wildlife Services predation management to protect wildlife ranged between $5,872,136 and $66,355,137.

Coyotes always have and always will feed on game animals, especially when they're available for the taking. The more of them there are, and the less there is of other prey in a given area, the more coyotes will prey upon them. Predation is a natural part of our ecosystem. When it all began, nature fully intended to use a balance scale with the predators there to control the numbers of other animals. However, humans have tipped the scales. Suburbanization, habitat destruction, and the introduction of additional predators such as domestic dogs and cats have upset the balance of predation and prey.

4

Trouble on the Home Front

QUESTION: *Why do people have problems with coyotes today?*

ANSWER: *Because coyotes are a nuisance to the other animals like chickens.*
        —Brittaney Webster, age 14

In previous chapters I discussed many wild natural foods of the coyote; however, I'm not so sure that only these foods are its natural diet. During the past century Wily has feasted upon various species of livestock, poultry, pets, melons and other fruits, garden vegetables, and garbage. His taste for all of these causes trouble on the home front, yet Wily has enjoyed our possessions for so long that they could now be considered his natural foods. In some areas young coyotes are even being taught to stalk and kill livestock, poultry, and pets more often than they're taught to kill rodents and other wild animals.

My questionnaire asked each state and province to name the number one complaint received about coyotes. Here's a rundown of what each agency that answered had to say:

Number One Complaint About Coyotes*

Alaska	None.
Arizona	Potential harm to pets.
California	Killing livestock and taking people's pets in urban and semiurban environments.
Delaware	Virtually no complaints.
Florida	Calves and goats (statewide). In some residential areas predation on pets has been a problem. Coyotes also do considerable damage to watermelon crops.
Georgia	Perceived impacts to native game species, especially deer, turkeys, and quail.
Idaho	Not available.
Illinois	Loss of livestock and pets.
Kansas	Livestock depredation.
Kentucky	Livestock damage.
Maine	Killing deer.
Michigan	People are concerned about hearing coyotes near their homes. There are fears about coyotes preying on pets (cats and dogs) and young children.
Minnesota	Urban nuisance.
Montana	Killing or harassing livestock (calves and lambs).
Nebraska	Livestock depredation.
New Brunswick	Killing deer/fawns.
New York	Perception of danger based on sightings, or hearing—and not knowing about them. "Will they hurt me?"

Number One Complaint About Coyotes* (Continued)

Northwest Territories	Very little (none known to me).
Nova Scotia	Sheep depredation.
Ohio	Sheep/livestock depredation.
Oklahoma	Livestock loss.
Oregon	Damage to livestock and pets.
Pennsylvania	Fear of coyotes.
Rhode Island	Seen in yards, and people wonder if they're dangerous.
South Carolina	General nuisance and fear. More calls are related to the fear the public has about the coyote than to depredation, primarily due to the general public's misunderstanding of the species.
South Dakota	Livestock depredation.
Utah	Livestock depredation.
Washington	Pets/livestock damage.
West Virginia	Sheep predation.
Wisconsin	Their presence. Most complaints are from the lack of understanding about coyote adaptability to humans and development. Complaints and concerns that evolve from this include fear of attacks on pets and children.
Wyoming	Livestock loss and the questionable perception of their impact on deer and antelope.

*As answered by 31 specialists in furbearers.

Surprisingly, Michigan, New York, Pennsylvania, and Wisconsin reported "fear" as the primary complaint about coyotes. Such fear is understandable, particularly in some areas where people may not be accustomed to seeing or hearing coyotes. As for Pennsylvania, a group of wildlife conservation officers was surveyed during December 1999 to determine the number of complaints filed and livestock lost to depredation by eastern coyotes. Of 251 complaints received, 45 percent cited a fear of coyotes. The state now suggests that a greater education effort is needed to inform the public about coyotes and their behavior.

Just how often a coyote will feast upon human property varies from area to area. Some coyotes have found it easier to enjoy a diverse diet of chickens, sheep, pets, and other animals raised by humans. No doubt it's less difficult to kill these animals than to kill wild ones. The diets of coyotes have been studied frequently to determine just how often they do feed upon human-raised animals. This is accomplished by examining scats and, in some cases, stomach contents.

Make no mistake, the coyote is truly a remarkable predator, but he's also a scavenger. He loves to kill and eat fresh meat, but he doesn't mind munching on the remains of an animal found dead, such as a deer lying in the woods, a cow sprawled out in a field, or a rabbit by the road that was crunched by an 18-wheeler. Wily is an opportunist. He takes advantage of any situation where he can stuff his gut with minimal risk. That's why his diet consists of so many different foods. When he lives close to humans, he may eat a few things that would surprise you.

Suburban Coyote Foods

In 1978 James MacCracken of the Department of Range Science at Colorado University conducted a study of coyote diets. His article, "Coyote Foods in a Southern California Suburb," published in the *Wildlife Society Bulletin,* provided valuable insight information on suburban coyotes' consumption of food specifically associated with human habitation.

MacCracken said that biologists, conservation officers, and the public became aware of increased coyote abundance in suburban southern California following the 1972 federal executive order banning the use of Compound 1080 (a poison used to kill coyotes). However, it was unknown if the coyotes invaded the suburbs from surrounding rangelands or the suburbs had expanded into traditional coyote ranges.

MacCracken's study area was located in a suburb of San Diego. The habitat consisted of foothills, steep hillsides, and numerous draws and valleys. Within the areas of native vegetation were clustered groups of homesites ranging from 5 to 20 years old. Intact coyote feces of all ages were collected in the area and individually bagged for analysis.

No less than 97 coyote feces were examined. It was presumed that this would represent coyote food habits throughout the year. Mammals accounted for 28.9 percent of the remains in scats examined. The most common mammals were cottontail rabbits, pocket gophers, blacktail jackrabbits, and house cats. Birds, predominantly chickens, accounted for 15.9 percent of identifiable remains. Vegetation comprised less than 22 percent of remains in scats (presumably from the stomachs of coyote's prey, and large pieces of grass). Seeds, fragments of chicken eggs, cellophane wrappers, pieces of cloth, string, plastic, and paper accounted for 16.7 percent of the remains in scats examined.

*Coyote Scat Contents**

Item	Percent of Frequency
Mammals	
Cottontail rabbit	12.1
Pocket gopher	6.8
Blacktail jackrabbit	2.3
House cat	2.3
Ground squirrel	1.5
Horse	1.5
Raccoon	0.8
Ringtail cat	0.8
Cow	0.8
Birds	
Chicken	8.3
Unidentified	6.8
Vegetation	
Plant fragments	10.3
Grass macrofragments	7.6
Unidentified fruit	3.0
Apple skin	0.8
Apple	0.8

Coyote Scat Contents* (Continued)

Item	Percent of Frequency
Miscellaneous	
Egg shell	3.8
Plastic	3.0
Cellophane wrapper	2.3
Cloth	2.3
String	2.3
Paper	1.5
Wood	1.5

*Percent frequency of occurrence of items recovered from 97 coyote feces collected from a southern California suburb (not all items found in coyote feces are shown here). Information courtesy of the Wildlife Society.

In his summary, MacCracken suggested that the principal foods of coyotes in his study have been reported to be major coyote foods in other parts of the western U.S.—rabbits and hares. In areas where rabbits and hares were scarce, other studies indicated that coyotes consumed voles and pocket gophers, whereas in Arizona, vegetation was frequently found in coyote feces. He also noted that these studies occurred where human influence was relatively minimal.

MacCracken added that another individual found that coyotes flourished in the presence of humans in Kansas. Chickens accounted for 14 percent of coyote foods in parts of Kansas where human influence was generally higher. The occurrence of house cats, apples, melon seeds, chickens, and garbage in coyote feces indicated that coyotes were capitalizing on the presence of humans. "The role that food items, specifically those associated with human settlement, play in coyote feeding strategies needs thorough examination if we are to fully understand the urban coyote's ecology and its relation to man," MacCracken stated.

Pets as Prey

Although MacCracken established that house cats are sometimes included in the coyote's diet, we can probably assume that coyotes eat them consistently in many human-populated areas of North America. Nature writer Dee Walmsley told me that 55 cat collars were discovered in a coyote den in Surrey, British Columbia, during the summer of 1999. Workers found the den while clearing brush on the edge of an urban forest as they widened the road. The incident occurred one block from Walmsley's home; she knew the den was there, often observing coyotes leaving it and going into the subdivision. At the time the den and cat collars were discovered, several lost-cat posters were hanging in the area.

Coyotes will kill and sometimes eat small dogs and puppies. Large dogs, such as shepherds, collies, and Labs, are seldom at risk. Once a coyote discovers how easy it is to prey upon pets, he's capable of cleaning out an entire neighborhood. Coyotes usually attack dogs only if they get too close to their den and pups, since they're very protective of their young. Then again, a coyote may satisfy his hunger pains by taking advantage of an easy situation.

According to a British Columbia Ministry of Environment fact sheet, an elderly woman took her small dog out for a walk in the city of Vancouver. A coyote appeared. Moments later the small dog became the coyote's prey. Another incident occurred in Geauga County, Ohio. A newspaper article reported that two dogs were savagely attacked by a coyote. Both dogs were outside, securely fastened with chains. One of them, a beagle hound, was found dead inside his doghouse with a large laceration on the neck. The other, a large collie, was attacked a few hundred yards away, but survived, suffering several bites and torn muscles. The individual who owned the beagle also had a cat mysteriously disappear a few months earlier. Although a larger dog could have been responsible for the maulings, officials believed it to be the work of a large coyote. In some places, such reports are common and probably wouldn't make the news, but pet maulings are much rarer in many urban areas.

Pets are considered easy prey for coyotes. Being raised by humans leaves them unsuspecting once they leave the safety of their pen or your home. Domestic cats and dogs have well-tuned senses, but they seldom rely on them because they don't anticipate being stalked, killed, and sometimes eaten by a predator such as Wily. In the wild, animals that don't rely on humans are dependent upon their senses for survival. Simply said, a coyote is much smarter, wiser, and more perceptive than any domesticated pet.

In many areas where coyotes are abundant, it's not unusual for people to be warned about their pets' safety. An article in an Arizona publication suggested that owners guard their pets, because dry weather had pushed many coyotes into a residential area. The article stated that one resident saw nine coyotes near a street corner when she went out on her nightly walk. Officials believed that the dry weather had reduced quality habitat and

The urban coyote is an opportunist—he'll feed upon a variety of animals and vegetation.

the coyote's natural food sources. Once this occurred, the predators headed for parks, particularly irrigated areas that might attract rodents, rabbits, and birds. Everyone was advised to keep their pets indoors in case a coyote might want to taste-test a dog or cat.

Wildlife conservation officers in Pennsylvania recorded coyote depredation of domestic livestock and pets during a 10-year period. There was a gradual increase in both. As for pets, none was documented as prey in 1988. One dog was preyed upon in 1989, and in 1990 three dogs and one cat became coyote prey. Coyotes preyed upon the highest number of cats in 1993 (24). In 1998 six dogs and five cats were killed by coyotes. The number of pets preyed upon isn't large by any means, but keep in mind that coyote populations only recently began expanding. You can also assume that the actual number of pets preyed upon is probably much higher, since missing pets often don't get classified as coyote prey.

You should understand that the coyote is not responsible for all missing and mutilated pets. If your pet comes up missing, or is found dead and perhaps partially devoured, you should not necessarily assume that Wily had anything to do with it. Wily probably wished he did, but he's not necessarily the guilty party. Some pets kill other pets. Foxes, bobcats, owls, and quite often anything with two or more wheels rolling down the sidewalk or road also kill pets.

Trash as Prey

Garbage! What more can I say. If you have read the book this far, you must know that a coyote would not pass up such an easy meal. Worse, as you will see in the following chapter, garbage is sometimes responsible for coyote attacks on humans. I'll provide a few solutions for garbage-eating coyotes later.

Fowl as Prey

I once enjoyed the company of several mallards near my rural home. The ducks spent most of their time on the dam of my pond, and eventually began raising ducklings. Once a coyote discovered their presence, he wasted no time in picking off one or two each night. That's how Wily works. Once he finds easy prey, he continues the assault until you stop him or there's no food left. The ducks, probably because they didn't have the sharp instincts of wild birds, did nothing on their own to stop the regular attacks. Only one hen survived. She finally left early one morning, only to return a couple of months later for a quick feeding. After the feeding, she flew away and we never saw her again.

People who raise fowl, be it ducks, geese, chickens, turkeys, or guineas, often find their birds disappearing on a nightly— and sometimes daily—basis. When coyotes attack poultry, they usually begin during the dark hours. If they are successful and nothing threatens them, they may begin showing up in daylight. More than likely, they will continue feeding on the poultry until the supply runs dry or until they're stopped.

Some commercial poultry raisers have made certain that coyotes can't get to the birds or eggs. Many people raise fowl just for the sheer enjoyment of having them around, however, and take few precautions to protect them. These folks often end up witnessing the aftermath of Wily's killing sprees. Seldom, though, can these folks be sure which predator is doing the dirty work. Lots of mammals, such as foxes, opossums, and raccoons; and raptors such as eagles, hawks, and owls will kill poultry. Again, I must point out that the coyote is not always to blame. Sometimes it's a cat, and sometimes man's best friend, as some folks call the dog. On one occasion I heard my chickens squawking, only to discover a free-roaming mutt on the scene. When I came out the door, he had the neck of my hen turkey clutched tightly in his mouth. I saved the turkey, but not before the dog had killed two chickens.

Every animal, including the coyote, has a distinct method of killing. Wily leaves telltale evidence on the scene. The methods he uses to kill and the evidence he leaves behind will be discussed in chapter 6.

Coyote in the Chicken Coop: Two Points of View

by Dee Walmsley, nature writer

I watch him as he approaches with his nose to the ground, his golden-tipped tail stretched to its fullest. He pauses, sniffs the air, ears twitching, turning, tuning in, then he continues on. The hen house sits 25 feet away. The last rays of sun are filling the sky with their pinky tones. The hens are settling in for the night, their squawky voices emanating through the walls as they jostle feathers perching in hay nests and rafter roosts.

A gust of wind catches a feather sending it twirling into the air. The coyote's golden eyes sparkle as he sits watching, waiting. The feather dances in the wind. The mangy critter cocks its head from side to side swaying to the rhythm of the dance. The wind moves on and the feather floats silently to the ground. Suddenly the coyote jumps into the air like a catapulted cat and pounces onto the feather, then just as quickly it loses interest and approaches the chicken-wire fence. Feet fly with the dirt as the digging begins, he pauses, catches his breath and shakes the dirt from the wetness of his nose, then continues his quest for chicken dinner. The chicken coop is silent.

"The air is cooling, must mean that it's sunset, dinner time. Guess I'll just mosey on over to farmer Brown's chicken coop and have a drumstick or two. Nuthin' like an evening's stroll to work up an appetite. Scratch, scratch, durn fleas is leaching the blood right out of me. Oh well, a little white meat will take my mind off them for a spell. Sniff, sniff, I can smell them in the air. Ah loves it when the wind blows, shuffles them flea varmints around too. What's thet whupped up thar? Ain't no bird. May as well set a minute and keep my eye on it, whatever it is. It's comin' down to ground, and it's all mine. C'mon bones spring ina action! Heck jus one of them feather things, best I git busy and stir up a few more of 'em. Cain't figger this out. Every time I dig a hole someone fills it in. Ah well nuthin' fore it but to dig another. Whew! I'm not the pup I use to be. Phooey, hate it when I gits a snout full o' dirt. Them hens know sumpthin' is up, just a couple more scratches and I'm in."

The coyote has stopped digging. He looks around then he lays flat on his belly, extends his front paws, disappears for a second and emerges from his tunnel on the other side of the wire fence. He is in the enclosure. He stands erect like a victor and proudly shakes the dust from his filthy coat. Stealthy like a thief in the night, he creeps towards the ramp leading into the chicken coop. He licks his chops in anticipation. The once magnificent tail twitches. Placing his two front paws on the ramp he slowly pulls his shoulders and head forward. His head enters the opening and all hell breaks loose. The chickens are heard squawking and fluttering within the coop. The coyote now has the front half of himself wedged into the doorway, his tail switching back and forth, hind legs pushing forward with all their might. An explosion rips through the air! The coyote shoots through the portal amidst a flurry of chickens. The hens exit into the enclosure two by two feathers flying. Somewhere a rooster crows as the farmer approaches the hen house.

Livestock as Prey

We can safely assume that many wilderness coyotes don't have access to livestock, poultry, fowl, pets, garbage, and other foods directly related to humans. On the other hand, we can also assume that many coyotes *are* within easy reach of people and their property. Several years ago I spent two weeks during the late summer on a Colorado ranch located in the high country of the Uncompahgre Plateau. The rancher had several head of sheep roaming a slope, all of which were subject to severe predation. One morning, after hiking two miles from the ranch, I discovered four sheep lying in a small meadow with their throats slashed. None of the sheep had been eaten. The rancher explained that this was a common summer scenario: The adult coyotes kill the sheep only to teach their pups how to kill. Although the resident coyotes often fed upon the sheep, it was the rancher's opinion they also killed just for the sake of preparing the youngsters for the future.

No doubt, sheep ranchers are quick to blame the coyote for all that he's responsible for, and for some things he isn't. They seldom look for sound evidence; it's easier to point the finger at North America's deadliest predator. Sometimes, however, a coyote will feed upon a dead sheep it didn't kill. When a sheep is found dead, eaten or not, many folks will still consider Wily the killer. Nonetheless, we cannot deny that he kills sheep (this has been witnessed on many occasions). They're easy to sneak up on, they're easy to kill, they're plentiful, they taste good, and they allow adult coyotes and pups to sharpen their hunting and killing skills. No, I don't really believe the coyote is innocent until proven guilty. On the other hand, who can blame the coyote for killing and eating livestock?

If you're not a rancher or an owner of livestock who has suffered losses due to coyote predation, you're probably feeling just a little bit sorry for these folks—but your feelings won't go overboard, because it isn't costing you moolah. Right? Wrong. If you're a taxpayer, it's costing you money, too. Yep, that's the way it works. In many cases, damages are assessed, and in some cases, those damages are paid back to the people who suffered losses. In many situations, officials are called in to investigate and control predation of livestock. These procedures also cost money.

Investigating any type of livestock damage, regardless of which animal is responsible, requires many hours of work. This costs money, usually paid to a local damage control agency, a state or provincial wildlife agency, and often the USDA. These costs exceed millions of dollars annually. For example, in 1993 Nova Scotia's Wildlife Investigation Report showed that personnel spent more than 8,000 hours and drove 220,000 kilometers investigating problems caused by wildlife. Granted, the total hours included all types of damage investigations caused by many species of animals, along with investigations that didn't end up involving damage. Nevertheless, you can bet that coyotes were responsible for some of the total hours.

From October 1, 1998, to September 30, 1999, Wisconsin Wildlife Services assisted in a large number of projects as a result of problems caused by wildlife. Coyotes accounted for 279 investigations, of which 79 were related to agriculture. Granted, this didn't compare to the 490 investigations due to Canada geese, or the 3,068 investigations of white-tailed deer, all of which were related to agriculture. Nonetheless, the coyote investigations did cost money.

In 1995 Montana sheep and lamb producers lost 92,000 head of livestock to weather, disease, predators, and other causes, according to a survey conducted by the Montana Agricultural Statistics Service. Predators, by the way, caused approximately two million dollars in losses. So just how often were coyotes the most costly predators? Wily and associates accounted for more than $1.5 million in losses.

Montana Sheep and Lamb Losses*

Predator	Total Losses	Value of Losses
Bears	300	$18,000
Coyotes	28,000	$1,513,400
Dogs	1,600	$101,400
Eagles	2,700	$138,500
Foxes	3,400	$166,100
Mountain lions	500	$31,100
Unknown	600	$32,600
Total Losses	**37,100**	**$2,001,000**

*1995 estimated Montana sheep and lamb losses due to predators. Statistics provided by Montana Agricultural Statistics Service.

Don't think for a minute that Montana stands alone when it comes to sheep and lamb losses due to coyote predation. A report published by the USDA's Agricultural Statistics Service showed 368,050 sheep and lambs were killed by predators in 1994 in the United States. Again, Wily and associates took top honors by capturing 66.2 percent of the total losses. Note: His close relative, the dog, finished second in the rankings.

To get an even better idea of costs, let me refer to *Economics of Wildlife Damage* once again. Bodenchuk, Mason, and Pitt surveyed livestock producers associated with the USDA-APHIS WS (Animal and Plant Health Inspection Service, Wildlife Services) program in 1998. These producers represent a cross section of livestock operators primarily in the 13 states of the WS western region, and are biased toward individuals with larger herds.

WS cooperators reported that predators killed approximately 22,600 cattle and calves, 144,000 sheep and lambs, and 35,000 goats and kids (excludes human children). You might not want to hear the market value, but I'll pass it along anyway. It was in excess of $17.4 million. This value is estimated for various reasons, but nonetheless it's astronomical. Officials say that opponents of predation management frequently claim that self-reported losses are sometimes exaggerated, but the available evidence suggests otherwise. Connolly (1992) reported that surveys of livestock producers tend to underreport loss, because reports emphasize confirmed kills. Additionally, the National Agricultural Statistics Service survey data typically report lower losses.

According to the National Agricultural Statistics Service, predation is the leading cause of sheep and lamb mortality. That comes as no big surprise. The annual rate of predation is 5.7 percent for adult sheep and 17.5 percent for lambs. Based on a 1999 National Agricultural Statistics Service report, predation losses averaged 1.6 percent of adult sheep and 6.0 percent of the calculated lamb crop when predation management programs were in place.

Goat production is growing in the Southwest. But goats are highly preferred by coyotes. In a two-year study of goat production in the absence of predation management, Guthery and Beasom (1978) reported that 49 percent of adult goats and 64 percent of goat kids were killed by predators in Texas. Shelton and Wade (1979) reported 100 percent of all kids and lambs were killed by predators during four short-term fencing tests in Texas. Overall predation rates on goats in these studies of loss in the absence of management exceeded 50 percent. Using predation management, the National Agricultural Statistics Service (1999) indicated that WS cooperators reported 12 percent of goats and kids killed by predators. Coyotes accounted for 42 percent of the kills.

The National Agricultural Statistics Service also estimates that coyotes account for 70.1 percent of cattle losses to predation. Using the Management Information System database, Utah Wildlife Services (1996) estimated that calf losses in the absence of predation management were 3.6 percent. That's a bit lower than other livestock. However, this may have been due to predation management to protect sheep that occurred in the same area. More broadly, the U.S. Department of the Interior (1978) reported that 85 percent of cattle producers in the Southwest lost no calves to coyote, 13 percent had losses of less than 5 percent, and 2 percent had losses of more than 5 percent. Because the majority of producers experiencing no loss were probably small operations, it's believed that the number of cattle actually lost to predation is somewhat higher than the preceding percentages.

As for direct costs, Bodenchuk, Mason, and Pitt said the true cost of predation management for one species is difficult to extract from Wildlife Services. Nonetheless, they estimated in those states with multiple predators, such as bears, bobcats, foxes, golden eagles, lions, and wolves, approximately 65 percent of the total predator losses can be attributed to coyotes. Additionally, they noted that coyotes represented 90 to 95 percent of the total animals removed to resolve damage complaints. Of 16 states in the West Region where livestock protection expenditures were calculated, Texas led the way with

$5,785,522. Expenditures in California and Montana exceeded $2 million. The total cost in the East Region was $502,813; Minnesota led the way in the East Region with a livestock protection expenditure of more than $200,000.

Predation on livestock continues to plague producers in the United States. According to Knowlton, Gese, and Jaeger, sheep inventories in the United States have declined more than 85 percent in the past 60 years, with a 25 percent decline between 1991 and 1996. The decline is attributed to low economic returns among producers, thanks to Wily and associates. They also pointed out that the magnitude and nature of predation can be misleading because of the varied nature of sheep operations, such as different sizes of operations, differences in management, and environmental circumstances surrounding individual operations. Coyote depredation rates appear to be influenced by sheep management practices, coyote biology and behavior, environmental factors, and depredation management programs, as well.

Cattlemen also take it on the nose when it comes to losses. For instance, the USDA reported that in 1995 predators killed 117,400 cattle in the United States (excluding Alaska). You guessed it—the coyote was the number one culprit.

The Minnesota Department of Natural Resources conducted a national study in 1993 to determine facts about wildlife damage in other states. Fifty questionnaires were sent to assess the types of damage, determine which animals were responsible, and collect other helpful facts. Forty-three states responded to the questionnaire, of which 23 said the coyote was the primary predator. The raccoon was ranked number one in nine states, the fox in eight states, and the mountain lion in three states. The principal damages coyotes caused ranged from livestock, poultry, and dog and cat losses to watermelon and aquaculture losses.

Coyote: The Number One Predator*

State	Damage #1	Damage #2
Alabama	Poultry	Cattle
Arkansas	Poultry	Cattle
Arizona	Cattle	Sheep
Georgia	Watermelon	Hog
Iowa	Sheep	Hog
Idaho	Sheep	None listed
Kansas	Sheep	Cattle
Louisiana	Aquaculture	Poultry
Massachusetts	Sheep	Dogs/cats
Maine	Sheep	Cattle
Michigan	Sheep	Poultry
Minnesota	Poultry	Sheep
Mississippi	Poultry	Cattle
Missouri	Poultry	Sheep
Montana	Sheep	Apiaries
Nebraska	Sheep	Cattle
Ohio	Sheep	Poultry
Rhode Island	Dogs/cats	Sheep

Tennessee	Poultry	Cattle
Texas	Sheep	Poultry
Utah	Sheep	Poultry
Virginia	Cattle	Poultry
Wyoming	Sheep	Horse

*Twenty-three states that named the coyote as their number one predator and the two primary types of damage caused by coyotes, as reported in 1993 by the Minnesota Department of Natural Resources in cooperation with the Minnesota Department of Agriculture.

Livestock predation goes back a long time. Stanley P. Young and Hartley H. T. Jackson reported that biological survey hunters examined the stomachs of about 30,000 coyotes between 1919 and 1923. More than 6,900 contained sheep or goat. Sheep and goat predation was somewhat seasonal, with the most frequent predation occurring from May through October. Other livestock, including horses, cattle, poultry, and hogs, were also found in the stomachs of coyotes. As for livestock consumption, beef ranked second while poultry ranked third. Another study of about 50,000 coyotes, which occurred from 1924 through 1928, produced very similar results.

Livestock predation can and does occur at any time of year, but research indicates that livestock is most susceptible to attack during the late spring and early summer, when coyotes are rearing pups.

Livestock owners also fear that when cows give birth, the afterbirth will attract coyotes. While this may be true some of the time, we also know that more coyotes feed upon the afterbirth than they do upon the calves. Many wild hoofed animals, such as deer, elk, and moose, will eat the afterbirth to avoid tempting a coyote or other predator.

Coyotes have also eaten the manure of newborn calves, probably to get the rich colostrum. Newborn calves (less than one week old) are sometimes preyed upon, but hungry coyotes seldom kill mature cows. A coyote may sit back and watch a cow and calf, only to move in on the calf when the mother walks away to feed. It's also possible that a calf will become a coyote meal just after the birthing process, since the mother cow could be too weak to fend off the predator.

When coyotes attack sheep, they usually approach the herd casually and circle it. When a sheep breaks away from the flock, a coyote will run it down and attack. Lambs are usually preferred, but all sheep are at risk. As are sheep, goats are particularly vulnerable to attack. It has been noted that Angora goats are especially vulnerable to coyote predation.

If you raise pigs, you may discover that a sow has become irritable. It could be that she has been losing piglets daily. A coyote will often sneak in and grab a piglet regularly until he gets them all, and in rare instances has snatched a piglet away from the sow while it nursed. Officials claim that coyotes seldom kill large pigs, although there are reports of coyotes killing pigs larger than 75 pounds.

A significant reduction in sheep losses occurred when predators were controlled during a study conducted by U.S. Department of the Interior. Researchers studied losses over a three year period on an 8,000-acre sheep ranch in Montana. During the first two years of the study, coyote damage was not controlled, and coyotes killed an average of 404 sheep each year. During the third year within a 1-mile buffer zone, predators were removed on the ranch with the help of Wildlife Services, USDA-APHIS. Damage control efforts cut the loss to 227 sheep—a 44 percent reduction in deaths from predation.

Coyotes living in ranch land clearly become dependent on animals raised by humans; however several factors influence depredation rates upon sheep, and sometimes other livestock. Knowlton, Gese, and Jaeger suggested that breeds, management practices, coyote behavior, and other pertinent factors should be considered. But let's look a little closer at coyote behavior.

Coyotes feed principally on small and medium-sized prey, such as rodents and rabbits, but they do learn to kill and feed on larger prey. Provisioning young is an important motivation for territorial coyotes to switch to killing lambs; however, this behavior appears to be reversible. When the pups were removed, the adults usually stopped killing sheep.

As they say, "there's always room for speculation." Some researchers suspect that coyote populations that aren't subject to human-induced mortality might pose less risk to livestock than populations manipulated to reduce coyote abundance. Thus, undisturbed coyote populations have fewer and smaller litters, resulting in reduced motivations to feed pups, which translates into reduced depredation of livestock.

On the other hand, one researcher reported that 41 percent of 34 kid goats were killed by coyotes within three weeks of their release within an unexploited coyote population with very low reproductive rates. No one knew which coyotes killed the goats (territorial or temporary coyotes), but both males and females fed on the goats. Another researcher reported significant predation on lambs in California during December and January, when coyote pups weren't present. This too indicates that removing pups isn't the only answer to coyote predation on lambs.

Eating Them Alive

Something else comes to mind when you think about coyotes preying upon a creature you've come to know. When coyotes prey upon livestock—pets or other prey, for that matter—do they kill the victim before feeding? Not always. Nevertheless, I would not hold this against Wily. The coyote does not see this as an act of merciless killing. He usually tries to do away with his prey first, as do many other predators, but the eating part is fun. So he often jumps the gun and begins eating as soon as he realizes the animal is down for keeps. This occurs most often when a pack of predators attacks an animal. You should be reminded, though, that animals don't fear death the way we do. They have a will to survive, but I must assume that they don't know when death is about to occur.

Unusual Damages

The coyote is not limited to predation upon livestock, poultry, and pets. In 1994 the USDA's ADC (Animal Damage Control), now WS (Wildlife Services), assisted officials at Tinker Air Force Base in Oklahoma when coyotes chewed through six fiber-optic lines that were to be used in maintenance of a B-1 bomber. Now, you might be wondering why a coyote would want to chew on fiber-optic lines, but as I said before, he is an opportunist. Maybe they tasted good, or maybe they came so easy that he couldn't pass them up. After the coyotes chewed the lines, they were considered damaged beyond repair. ADC captured two coyotes and made certain that other lines would not be damaged.

On many occasions the Lake Tahoe Airport experiences coyote obstacles. They cause all kinds of confusion and delays, especially when they lie on the runway to sun themselves, or move about in search of food. Sometimes they dart across the runway in front of moving planes (although to my knowledge they haven't been chasing planes and biting at the tires). The airport has considered repairing the current fence, installing a new fence, and closing off drainpipes, where they often den and raise pups.

You've probably noticed high fences around some airports. Many animals, including coyotes, often become pests around airports and threaten human safety. Back in the 1980s a pilot from Dallas, Texas, reported coyotes on the runway when he took off from there, and a coyote on the runway in Dayton, Ohio, where he landed. Fortunately, his experiences passed without incident. Surprisingly, though, coyotes have damaged landing gear when they were hit by moving planes. On rare occasions they have also been thrown into the engines of airplanes.

Wily Loves Fruit

Few people realize just how much a coyote likes melons and other fruits. Wherever melons are grown, there's apt to be a few lying with their guts spilled out on the ground. Again, though, this is nothing new. Stanley P. Young and Hartley H. T. Jackson said that a melon grower in Imperial County, California, reported that coyotes were destroying a large share of his 200 acres of melons in September 1944. The coyotes had feasted upon 1,500 pounds of melons during a one-week period, just when they were about to turn pink, or ready for human consumption. At that time they were valued at 5½ cents per pound.

As for other fruits, coyotes love eating apricots, cherries, grapes, peaches, plums, pumpkins, and mesquite beans (the fruit of a common bush in southwestern deserts). Many folks might not think that this is a serious problem, but those who raise these fruits are aware that the coyote's appetite for them has cost them plenty of money.

Urban Concerns

It's difficult to say exactly where the coyote is the biggest pest. Many rural folks have certainly had their share of trouble with Wily. To many folks, though, it might seem that the worst problems are in the urban areas and suburbs, where Wily is often spotted coexisting with people.

Many people in these areas have limited knowledge of coyotes, according to Kristine Lampa, who surveyed residents of Vancouver, British Columbia. In 1995 and 1996 she conducted two surveys that questioned attitudes and concerns about urban wildlife. The first survey polled Vancouver community centers, and the second was directed to the general population, veterinary clients, and naturalists. She concluded that because of a lack of wildlife education, many people not only express negative opinions about coyotes, but they also often fear them.

Several questions were asked in the two surveys. In one survey the first question asked that the respondent place an "X" by

Wily can make himself comfortable anywhere—even this urban parking lot.

any species of animals that they considered to be urban wildlife (24 species were listed). Surprisingly, 84 percent of the respondents said coyotes were urban animals, along with a number of smaller animals such as squirrels and raccoons. When asked to name "urban pests," coyotes were again identified, along with Canada geese, raccoons, mice, and rats. However, there was quite a difference in the number of people (70 percent) who said rats were an urban pest, and those (29 percent) who named the coyote as an urban pest.

As for why a particular species caused people to worry, most noted that "the safety of children and personal safety" were their primary concerns. Property damage was next in line, while the safety of pets ranked third.

The urban folks who responded to Lampa's surveys had every right to be concerned. In fact, 82 percent of the residents surveyed were aware that coyotes were present in Vancouver. Forty-two percent had seen a coyote locally during the previous two years, and 27 percent said they thought coyote numbers were increasing. No less than 70 percent believed that coyotes were present in the city because "we have taken over the coyote's habitat."

As for the survey respondents understanding the coyote's diet, many were on track. More than 80 percent believed that coyotes would prey on domestic pets (they were right). However, 22 percent believed that coyotes were active and hunting only at night. They were wrong.

Lampa determined that wildlife in the Vancouver area enhances the residents' quality of life, and that wildlife heightens the enjoyment of outdoor recreation experiences. Based on the surveys, she and others developed an educational approach to address public concerns and misconceptions about coyotes. Lampa suggested that the surveys identified these four factors:

1) Coyotes are of genuine concern to the public.
2) An educational approach is favored in dealing with concerns about urban wildlife.
3) The public has specific concerns about coyotes.
4) There are gaps in the public's knowledge about coyotes.

After all I have said in this chapter about Wily and the rest of the coyotes in North America, you may have a different opinion than you had before, or it may have remained the same. Most folks tend to judge the coyote by their own experiences with him. If a coyote has not yet caused you a problem, you probably don't care one way or the other.

Here's how it works: You will probably enjoy the howling sounds of a coyote, unless the music is 50 yards away from the chicken coop. You will smile when a coyote darts across a hillside near dusk on a cool evening, unless your sheep are on the same hillside. You won't mind stopping your vehicle near the city park to let a coyote pass, unless the mangled body of your beloved pet was found the day before in the same park. You'll also love the documentary on television about coyotes as you sit back on the sofa and enjoy popcorn and a cold soda pop, unless you just returned home from a long hike where you witnessed the screaming bleats of a newborn deer fawn, just after a coyote grabbed it by the throat.

5

Human-Coyote Confrontations

QUESTION: What would you do if you saw a coyote coming toward you?

ANSWER: I would run if it was old, but if it was a baby, I would just walk away.
                    —Jessica Webster, age 12

ANSWER: I would just stand still and I wouldn't move.
                    —Brittaney Webster, age 14

Before scaring your socks off, let me first say that coyotes rarely attack people. You'll probably call me a liar after reading the rest of this chapter, but I base these words on the human population living in and near coyote habitat, and the great number of coyotes that have taken up residence in urban districts.

Unfortunately, there are no lump sum statistics available that would let us all know just how many people have been attacked by coyotes, or how much money these attacks have cost taxpayers. There's no national database waiting to print as soon as someone clicks the mouse on the right icon. But there are reports available in scattered locations throughout North America, and I was able to gather some interesting details about attacks on humans. There have been a number of incidents in recent times, most of them in human-inhabited areas; however, dogs attack far more people than do coyotes.

Dog bites are much more serious than coyote attacks on humans, according to the State Farm Insurance Company's Web site (www.statefarm.com). The site reported that dog-bite victims requiring medical attention in the United States number 500,000 to 1 million annually. Sixty percent of them are children. Next in line, and also at great risk, are mail carriers and meter readers. The Web site also reported that every 40 seconds someone in the United States seeks medical attention for a dog bite, costing insurance companies more than a billion dollars per year.

Enough said about dogs, though. Let's get on with 10 facts about coyotes that attack humans.

1. Coyotes attack more children than adults.
2. Coyotes aren't particularly eager to bite mail carriers and meter readers.
3. Coyotes don't bite 500,000 to 1 million people annually.
4. A coyote doesn't attack a human every 40 seconds, or every 40 minutes.
5. Most coyotes that attack people don't carry rabies.
6. Most coyote attacks are incidental and weren't planned by the coyote.
7. When a coyote does attack, a solitary animal is often responsible.
8. Coyote attacks on humans don't cost insurance companies a billion dollars per year, but they have cost them money.

9. Most attacks occur in areas where coyotes frequently encounter people.
10. Many documented attacks have occurred in parks where no hunting is allowed, and near parks where coyotes lose their fear of humans.

If you're wondering if a coyote has ever attacked a human in your state or province, you may know with certainty after reading the details of several attacks that follow. Or you may want to glance at the accompanying table to see how state and provincial specialists answered my questionnaire.

Coyote Attacks by State or Province

State or Province	Coyote Attacks on Humans?
Alaska	"Not that we're aware of."
Arizona	"Yes."
California	"Yes."
Delaware	"No."
Florida	"No."
Georgia	"We are unaware of any documented reports."
Idaho	"Unknown."
Illinois	"Not to our knowledge."
Kansas	"Not that we're aware of."
Kentucky	"Not to our knowledge."
Maine	"No."

(Continued)

Coyote Attacks by State or Province (Continued)

State or Province	*Coyote Attacks on Humans?*
Michigan	"Not to the best of our knowledge—people should be more concerned about domestic dogs and pets."
Minnesota	"No."
Montana	"Not to our knowledge."
Nebraska	"Not to our knowledge."
New Brunswick	"Yes."
New York	"Not to our knowledge—only a matter of time."
Northwest Territories	"We don't think so."
Nova Scotia	"One incident that we're aware of."
Ohio	"No recorded attacks on people."
Oklahoma	"Not to our knowledge."
Oregon	"Not to our knowledge."
Pennsylvania	"Yes."
Rhode Island	"None recorded or reported."
South Carolina	"Not to our knowledge."
South Dakota	"None that we're aware of."
Utah	"Unsure."
Washington	"Unsure."
West Virginia	"No."
Wisconsin	"No."
Wyoming	"No."

Of the 31 states and provinces that responded to the questionnaire, only 5 said coyotes had attacked a human. However, only seven answered "no." Some were unsure, and many weren't aware of any attacks.

Despite the unlikeliness that a coyote will attack, I think it best to get on with the details of some of the attacks that have occurred in North America. These are not what you would call bedtime stories. Nonetheless, they are the most effective ways to explain why, how, when, and where coyotes are most likely to attack humans.

While playing on a swing set in the backyard of his home in a residential area of Sandwich, Massachusetts, a three-year-old boy was attacked by a coyote in July 1998. His sister, who was also playing on the swing, alerted their mother that a coyote had run across the yard, knocked the boy down, and then attempted to drag him away while biting him.

When the mother arrived on the scene, she began beating and kicking the coyote in hope that he would abandon the attack. The coyote did let go of the boy; however, he remained only 3 feet away, bluff charging the mother while she held her son in her arms, possibly hoping to make her drop the boy. Finally, she managed to force the coyote far enough away to get into the house. When she went back outside to get her daughter, the coyote was again on the way to the swing set. The woman yelled and threw toys at the coyote to get him to move farther away so she could retrieve the child.

The boy was taken to a hospital with puncture wounds from the coyote's teeth, along with scratches and abrasions. He was treated and eventually released to his home to recover. Fortunately, he didn't have to undergo a series of injections for rabies.

After the attack, the coyote lingered in the backyard. Police soon arrived on the scene and disposed of the animal. It was later reported that the coyote had been prowling neighborhoods near the Otis Air National Guard Base in the weeks preceding the attack. The police department and Animal Control had received several reports of a coyote that was acting "bold and aggressive." Several cats had also been reported missing, and Animal Control had reported finding the remains of cats in the area. The attack occurred approximately 2 miles outside the centralized area of reports. The police department noted that the reports ceased the day after they removed the coyote.

The Department of Public Health later examined the head of the coyote. The animal tested negative for the rabies virus. Preliminary results showed the coyote was an adult male, weighing 40 pounds. He also had a healed fracture on his right foreleg. A doctor suggested the injury had occurred more than one year earlier. Some people believed someone may have treated the coyote's leg, but this speculation was never proven.

Division biologists immediately went to work on determining why the animal was seen regularly in the Sandwich neighborhood. According to Susan Langlois, furbearer biologist, food could have been the lure, although no evidence suggested humans had fed the coyote. The coyote may have been looking for handouts, or his injury might have prevented him from hunting and scavenging naturally. Langlois added that a sudden movement or noise could trigger a coyote attack, even if food isn't an issue.

Yellowstone National Park has experienced a few coyote attacks, too. In the late 1960s a coyote in the Mammoth area in Yellowstone attacked a nine-year-old girl as she walked to school. She was knocked to the ground and bitten on the leg.

Because this coyote seemed to have little fear of humans, Yellowstone National Park officials moved it from a people-populated picnic area to a remote location.

In 1974 a photographer was busy filming a geyser in Yellow-stone when a coyote lunged at him from ten feet away. The man kicked at the coyote and knocked it away, but it continued lung-ing toward him. It gave up only when the man's foot sank into the underside of its jaw, causing it to bite its tongue. Later the man learned that the coyote had attacked his partner while he was unloading equipment.

In January 1990 a coyote lunged at a man skiing, knocking him off his feet. As the man lay on the ground, the coyote at-tacked his face. He escaped only after he managed to hit it in the head with one of his skis. The man received several punc-ture wounds and a trip to the hospital.

In 1995 a coyote grabbed a toddler from his yard in Los Alamos, New Mexico. Again, the mother saved the child. She heard her son's screams and ran outside just in time to see the coyote dragging him away. Her aggression soon forced the coyote to abandon the thought of eating the child.

In October 2000 a Mesa, Arizona, boy was bitten by a coyote and almost dragged away. His father had just come home with groceries, put the 22-month-old child down, and walked into another room. He then heard his son scream. When he looked, he saw a coyote holding the boy in its mouth trying to carry him outside the house through an open door. As soon as the coyote saw the father, it dropped the boy and ran.

The next day the father shot a 27-pound coyote in his yard. Officials believe it may have been the same animal that had attacked the boy, but area Game and Fish Department officials continued searching the area for three packs of coyotes, one of which had been acting strangely. It was believed that the coyote looked in the house, spotted the boy, and decided he was an easy target. Unfortunately, the toddler had to undergo a series of rabies shots.

Kristine Lampa, in her thesis "Urban Coyotes in the Lower Mainland, British Columbia: Public Perceptions and Education," discussed brief details of two coyote attacks on children that occurred in 1995 and 1997 in the greater Vancouver area in British Columbia. In both cases, two children, one age three and one age seven, while in the presence of an adult, were approached by a coyote. Neither attack was serious, and health department officials did not see a need for rabies treatment. Both incidents occurred in Burnaby Park, but nobody knows if the same coyote was responsible for both. After the second attack, a single coyote was removed from the area. Food was not known to be a positive factor in the coyote's aggression, but it's possible that a local resident was feeding the coyote in the park, which may have encouraged its bold behavior.

Arizona voters banned trapping on public land a few years ago. Many claim this has led to an increase in the number of coyotes invading urban areas in the state. In the early 1990s coyotes attacked two children in a metropolitan area of Phoenix. Dr. Bill Morill, a wildlife biologist and the Safari Club's conservation director, said conflicts between humans and coyotes in urban areas underscore the way coyotes can adapt to living anywhere. Dr. Morill observed, "Coyotes have discovered that living in cities means plenty of cover, escape routes, and food. But it also can mean that a child or an adult who gets between a coyote and trash, or a dog food bowl, can become the target of a coyote intent on getting its meal."

A Fredericton, New Brunswick, newspaper received a letter to the editor. The letter writer told about a coyote that showed little fear of people and was consuming available garbage in the urban area. The individual spotted the coyote after leaving a movie theater. He followed the coyote to the backside of a local business, where it began eating garbage; he also noticed that the canine had clumps of hair hanging off it everywhere. Surprisingly, the coyote didn't mind people hanging around it, watching it feed. It was also reported that some of the youngsters watching the coyote believed it to be a dog.

In February 2000 a coyote bit a teenage girl who was vacationing at the home of her grandmother in Deer Island, New Brunswick. While out with her boyfriend, she stopped not far from the house to answer the call of nature. It was dark, and she didn't know a coyote had sneaked up on her until the predator bit her on the hip. At first she thought she'd bumped into a bramble bush, but when she turned, she spotted a four-legged animal running away. She returned to the vehicle and explained to her boyfriend what had happened. He turned the car toward the area where she had been bitten, and they spotted a coyote lying on the ground 50 feet from where the incident occurred. When the boy got out of the car, the canine ran away. The girl had to undergo rabies shots.

In 1992 a Dauphin County, Pennsylvania, maintenance crew was clearing brush when one of them spotted an injured deer. As the man approached the deer, he saw blood on the animal. Curious and concerned, the man followed the deer, only to be surprised by a coyote. The coyote grabbed the man and bit him on the leg before being scared away. It was believed that the coyote had attacked the deer and was in pursuit of it. It may have attacked the man in an effort to protect its prey.

In 1990 a Vermont bowhunter was attacked by a coyote while deer hunting. Officials could not explain the attack, except to say that the coyote may have been attracted to the fox-scented clothing the hunter wore. Coyotes tend to hate foxes.

California has certainly had its share of coyote problems, and when it comes to attacks on humans, the numbers are high. In July 1997 a three-year-old Palo Alto boy and his family were getting ready to head home after a picnic at Windy Hills Open Space Preserve. A coyote rushed out of the bushes, grabbed the youngster by the hand, and began dragging him into the bushes. The boy's brother scared the coyote away, and the boy was transported to a hospital. He was treated for wounds on his head and hands.

After the attack, officials closed trails. Meanwhile, in the same area, a wildlife specialist set rubber traps that would not harm coyotes. The trap caught a coyote, which would soon go on trial. The investigation began with a Frisbee the boy had been playing with at the time of the attack, which was also bitten by the coyote. A DNA sample of the Frisbee was taken to see if it would match the DNA of the trapped coyote.

Several other coyote attacks occurred in California from 1988 to 1997. Rex O. Baker of the Horticulture/Plant and Soil Science Department, California State Polytechnic University, and Robert M. Timm of the Hopland Research and Extension Center, University of California, did their homework by gathering the details of the attacks. Additionally, the two men provided information about the coyotes—before attacks occurred. In some cases they even discussed the methods that resolved the problem. Here are the details of a few of the incidents that appeared in their article "Management of Conflicts Between Urban Coyotes and Humans in Southern California":

- San Diego, San Diego County, 1988: A 24-year-old woman was approached and bitten by a coyote in the urban area of San Diego while talking on a cellular phone in her backyard. Neighbors in the area reported recent sightings of coyotes boldly wandering in the area. A resident two houses away had lost a small dog to a coyote, and three or four cats in the neighborhood had similarly been taken. The Animal Damage Control (ADC) specialist who responded to the complaint removed the offending coyote within less than a week by use of a leghold trap in the woman's yard. No further incidents were reported.

- Reds-Mountain Campground, Madera County, 1990: A
  five-year-old girl in a sleeping bag was attacked and bitten
  during the early morning of June 29, 1990. The campground is about 6 miles west of Mammoth Lakes in the
  Inyo National Forest. Adults sleeping near the child,
  awakened by the child's screams, saw the coyote retreat.
  The child sustained a severe scalp laceration and several
  canine puncture wounds, and she received medical treatment. USDA-ADC personnel and others, working in
  cooperation with U.S. Forest Service and Park Service
  personnel, shot four coyotes in the vicinity. Interviews
  with park rangers and campground residents revealed
  that people in the area had been feeding coyotes. It was
  also noted that skiers at Mammoth Mountain, only a few
  miles away, had been feeding coyotes during the winter
  ski season. Observers noted that coyotes would readily
  approach people for food, showing little fear. The investigation also revealed two previous biting incidents had
  occurred the same day. One person was bitten on the foot
  through a sleeping bag, while another individual was bitten on the hand.
- San Clemente, Orange County, 1992: The attack on a
  child was preceded by three to four weeks of coyote attacks on two dogs and six house cats, as reported to San
  Clemente Animal Control (Gene Begnell, San Clemente
  City Fire Department/Animal Regulation, pers. comm.).
  All of the attacks were in the same residential area, and
  coyotes were readily seen day and night, especially on
  trash-collection days. One licensed child-care facility reported having to bring children inside from the rear yard,

which faced a common landscaped slope, due to a coyote
stalking the children's play area. This facility was about ¼
mile from the nearest wildlife fringe area. The five-year-
old girl who was bitten attempted to escape from the coyote by climbing onto a swing set. The child's mother
scared off the coyote, but the girl sustained several bites
on her back. Police tried to shoot coyotes for several
nights following the attack, but failed to take any coyotes.
Two coyote dens and numerous bedding areas were found
in the landscaped slope areas throughout the development. Trapping was conducted for 10 days by Animal Pest
Management (APM), resulting in removal of six coyotes,
primarily adults. APM biologists shot another two coyotes.
Coyotes have not been a problem since the control program. When seen, they are now on outer fringe areas and
run to avoid humans.

- Oceanside, San Diego County, 1988: Three children were
  approached or bitten in separate events on August 16, 17,
  and 18, 1988, in the Oceano, Hermosa, and Peacock Hills
  area of Oceanside. In the three weeks prior to these
  events, USDA-ADC personnel had received 30 to 40 complaints of coyotes attacking or killing household pets, or
  approaching people during daylight hours in the Oceanside area. During approximately the same time period,
  the commanding brigadier general of the adjacent Camp
  Pendleton Marine Base had reported that coyotes harassed his wife and threatened the family's dog.
- In one incident, when an eight-year-old girl fell while
  roller skating, a coyote ran at her and grabbed her skate.
  Two women chased the animal away by throwing rocks at

it. In a second incident, a four-year-old boy playing in the front yard of his grandfather's home received a bruise when a coyote nipped him on the knee. In a third incident, three-year-old Jessica Lee, while playing in her grandfather's driveway, was grabbed on the leg by a coyote that pulled her down, biting her on the leg, neck, and head. Her mother and neighbors screamed at the coyote and chased it away. During the week following the three incidents involving children, an ADC Specialist removed three coyotes from the area, two by use of leghold traps and one by shooting. One of the trapped coyotes was found to be suffering from distemper. No further coyote attacks on humans were reported.

- University of California, Riverside County, 1995: On the campus of the University of California Riverside (UCR), cat remains were found numerous times during the two to three months prior to the first attack on children. It was discovered that residents of the campus family housing area had been leaving feed out for feral cats. Coyotes were seen chasing and carrying off cats at night and early in the morning. By late spring coyotes were observed feeding on cat food in the afternoon, and had occasionally chased joggers on rural trails. In June three boys in the housing area were chased out of a playground by a coyote that eventually caught and bit a seven-year-old boy. Between the first attack at UCR (June 1995) and the second one (November 1995), adults accompanied the children to the playground, and some children stayed closer to home. Coyote activity increased during daylight hours on and near the campus. A coyote even appeared on a soccer field during a game attended by numerous fans. More joggers and cyclists reported being chased near a heavily landscaped area.

- After the second child was attacked, a site evaluation revealed pet food left out for one or two remaining cats, and areas of exposed garbage and trash were identified. Officials also found numerous rabbit remains around several shrub and lawn areas, and coyote feces. The feces were examined and found to contain rabbit, skunk, roof rat, fruit, trash, and cat and dog food. Of necessity, shooting was restricted to a very limited area that was deemed a safe shooting zone, and which was out of public sight. Recorded urban animal cries, as well as the call of a distressed cottontail, were again used to attract the coyotes. Only two adult coyotes were taken using firearms. Leghold traps were successfully used to remove an additional five coyotes. Now, over two years later, no more attacks or harassment has occurred, although feral cats have started to populate the campus again. No coyotes have been spotted on campus in daylight hours, but occasionally one is seen at a distance at night in the native plant garden area and in adjacent brush on the east side of campus. Some of the trapped coyotes came from the freeway right-of-way, and others traveled on the railroad right-of-way from wildland habitat about ¼ mile to the east.

- Newport Beach, Orange County, 1994: Neighborhood attacks on domestic animals and pets over a six-month period preceded the July 1994 incident where a mother rescued her two-year-old child that was being stalked by a coyote. Neighbors near Upper Newport Bay reported seeing coyotes with no apparent fear of humans, foraging in neighborhoods and yards during daylight hours. The mother screamed and ran out of the house to rescue her toddler, after seeing a coyote apparently crouched for attack 5 feet away from her son. She had lost 23 chickens and 22 rabbits to coyotes in her backyard during the preceding months, and coyotes had killed a neighbor's German shepherd. City animal control authorities recommended residents take steps to remove coyote food sources, and they initiated an effort to shoot the offending coyotes.

- Laguna Nigel, Orange County, 1991: This case involved a pet owner who had his poodle taken out of his arms by an attacking coyote. The poodle was not saved. Coyotes had been seen in early and late mornings chasing and killing cats and rabbits in the neighborhood prior to the attack. After this incident, several coyotes were taken with padded leghold traps and euthanized, and there has been no reoccurrence of problems at this site (the 1995 incidents in Laguna Nigel were in a different neighborhood and are considered unrelated).

- South Lake Tahoe, El Dorado County, 1997: In February 1997 late-morning coyotes' activity had been reported at a ski lodge parking lot and in nearby neighborhoods. A man was bitten while actually feeding a coyote in the parking lot of a ski lodge. A four-year-old girl was attacked in the yard of a South Lake Tahoe residence where she was staying with her family. She was largely protected by the heavy snowsuit she was wearing, but she suffered multiple wounds to her face. Sixteen of the wounds required stitches. The coyote had to be pulled off the child by the father, and it would still not leave after being hit. It appeared to stay "locked on" its prey until it was shot by a sheriff. Coyotes had been fed by a homeowner within a short distance of the site of the attack.

- San Clemente, Orange County, 1997: The attack did not result in an injury because the parents, who have been prevented from putting up a coyote-proof fence by their homeowners association, only let the two-year-old child play outdoors when they were with her. The coyote boldly approached the child, who was with her father and another man working on a backyard deck. It was seen a few feet away in a "freeze mode," seemingly locked onto the child as a prey item, and crouched for attack when the father grabbed the child. Had the child moved, the coyote most likely would have attacked, since movement is a key stimulus for initiating attack.
- Trapping was initiated by APM, and several coyotes were removed by use of traps in the same yard. A compost pile and vegetable garden in the yard were used by the coyotes as food sources. Most feces collected in the area had a high occurrence of seeds of *Ficus nitida,* a street tree that produces a mass of berry-sized fruit. In addition to plant material, fragments of house cat, cottontail rabbit, and small rodents, and pet food were found in coyote scats.

Baker and Timm documented coyote attacks on 53 people in 16 locations, resulting in 21 bites, and 32 individuals that were harassed over the nine-year period in California. Here's a brief look at a few more of those cases:

Verified Coyote Attacks in California, August 1988 to September 1997*

Date	Victim	Details
Aug. 1988	8-year-old girl	Coyote tugged at her skate while she was roller skating.
Aug. 1988	4-year-old boy	Nipped and bruised by coyote while playing in yard.
Oct. 1994	Adult male	Man with no shirt or shoes bitten by coyote.
Mar. 1995	Adult male	Man with no shirt bitten by coyote.
June 1995	Adult female	Woman in shorts and no shoes, preparing food, bitten by coyote.
July 1995	Adult male	Man bitten by coyote while sleeping in lawn (2:45 P.M.).
July 1995	Adult male	Man bitten by coyote while sleeping in lawn (4:00 P.M.).
July 1995	15-month-old girl	Coyote returned to attack infant in jumpsuit after being chased away once; child suffered bites to leg.
June 1995	6 adults and children	All chased from patio table by coyote. Despite the yelling of adults to frighten the animal, all chicken dinners were taken and eaten by the coyote.
June 1995	Adult male	Man lying on lounge bitten on foot by coyote while stargazing.
June 1995	Adult male	While getting paper in yard, man bitten on bare foot by coyote.

Verified Coyote Attacks in California, August 1988 to September 1997* (Continued)

Date	Victim	Details
Jan. 1997	Adult female	Coyote assaulted woman, grabbed lunch pail, and ran.
Jan. 1997	Adult female	Coyote charged woman and grabbed her purse containing lunch.
Jan. 1997	Adult male	Coyote attacked man and bit shoe; no injury. Coyote refused to retreat.
Jan. 1997	Adult male	Coyote jumped on back of man, biting his backpack.
Sept. 1997	Adult male	Man stalked and attacked by two coyotes, then bitten on ankle.

*Not all of the attacks that were documented are shown in this table.

Baker and Timm noted that many areas surrounding the suburbs are attractive to rodents and other animals that attract coyotes. For instance, community plans and government ordinances, for aesthetic and noise-reduction purposes, have changed freeways and streets into beautiful landscapes. These areas attract rabbits, pocket gophers, ground squirrels, and meadow mice within one to two years after planting, all of which are commonly part of the coyote's diet. There are also drainages in the nearby canyons and brushy habitats scattered about. Thus, the coyote has food, water, and cover.

Baker and Timm reported that coyote attacks on humans are no longer rare or unusual in many California urban fringe areas. They added that during the last decade, Californians have seen a major increase in the number of reported coyote attacks on children, adults, and pets. None of the attack cases involved a rabies-positive coyote, however. Baker and Timm added, "Public awareness of the danger of coyotes and other large predators to humans and pets was found to remain a limited and localized issue, primarily existing where prior problems had occurred. The general public's lack of concern and awareness is a serious problem and is the real root of coyote-human conflicts."

Although none of the cases investigated by Baker and Timm involved rabies, they did note that this disease is endemic to much of the United States, including California. If rabies becomes more prevalent in coyotes in urban areas, there could be severe public health consequences because of the high risk of contact between coyotes and people, or their pets.

Baker and Timm only documented attacks reported by more than one reputable source, and preferably by a city, county, or state agency, or of which they had personal knowledge. Not included in their article were numerous other reports of pets being torn out of people's arms, cyclists being knocked over, chased, or both, and joggers being nipped at by coyotes. They said park rangers also reported the reluctance of some people to file reports after being attacked by coyotes.

Los Angeles County, California, has also had its share of coyote threats and attacks on humans that involved one death. A report from the Department of Agricultural Commissioner and Weights and Measures documented 15 incidents from 1975 to 1995. Here's a look at the details:

Reported Attacks or Harassment by Coyotes on Humans Within Los Angeles County*

Location	Date	Details
Glendale	Feb. 6, 1975	A lost 2-year-old boy was found surrounded by a pack of coyotes. He was rescued by Glendale police.
Glendale	August 1981	A 3-year-old girl was killed by a coyote in her front yard—neck broken, massive bleeding.
Glendale	July 19, 1982	A teenage girl was tracked by a coyote while jogging.
Agoura	July 1980	A 13-month-old girl was grabbed and dragged off by a coyote. She received puncture wounds to her midsection. Saved by her mother.
Pasadena	May 1978	A 5-year-old girl was bitten on her left leg by a coyote while in the driveway of her home.
Pasadena	May 1979	While eating cookies on her front porch, a 2-year-old girl was grabbed by a coyote by her throat and cheek.
Pasadena	June 1979	While picking up the newspaper in his yard, an adult male was bitten on the heel by a coyote.
Pasadena	July 1979	A 17-year-old girl had her leg torn by coyotes while attempting to save a dog that was under attack.
Pasadena	July 1979	A coyote bumped the legs of a male jogger. The man climbed a tree to escape.

(Continued)

Reported Attacks or Harassment by Coyotes on Humans Within Los Angeles County* (Continued)

Location	Date	Details
Pasadena	Oct. 28, 1984	A 21-year-old security guard at Art Center College was bitten on the hand while fleeing 8 to 10 coyotes pursuing him. The man was confronted while eating a sandwich.
La Verne	Aug. 1979	A coyote grabbed a 5-year-old girl and attempted to drag her into bushes. She received deep bites on her neck, head, and legs, but was saved by her father.
Acton	May 16, 1982	A male teenager was attacked and bitten on his left hand while jogging.
Covina	July 2, 1982	A 52-year-old Forest Lawn Cemetery worker reported being attacked by a coyote while on a mowing tractor. The coyote missed the man's foot and bit a rear tire.
Burbank	Aug. 5, 1982	A six-year-old was bitten on the thigh while playing in her front yard on BelAire Drive.
Los Angeles	July 20, 1995	A 15-month-old girl from Nevada was bitten on the thigh at Griffith Park, near the merry-go-round. The coyote released her when confronted by the mother.

*Each incident came from one of the following sources: police department reports; Pasadena Department of Human Services animal bite reports; news media; Los Angeles County chief medical examiner—coroner; or personal interview. Compiled by County of Los Angeles, Department of Agricultural Commissioner and Weights and Measures.

An article by Ludwig N. Carbyn of the Canadian Wildlife Service, "Coyote Attacks on Children in Western North America," published by the Wildlife Society, details several coyote attacks between 1960 and 1988. Carbyn summarized information from warden reports in Banff and Jasper National parks, located in the Canadian Rocky Mountains, western Alberta, and in Yellowstone National Park in Montana and Wyoming. He summarized the attacks in one of four categories:

1. *Preliminary investigations*—situations where coyotes probably lost fear of humans and approached with apparent intent to attack. No evidence of further actions was noted after the initial attempts.

2. *Persistent investigations*—attacks where there were repeated attempts to approach an intended victim, but no physical contact was made.

3. *Minor attacks*—coyotes made physical contact with humans, including biting. Wounds were not life threatening, but without defense could have been more serious.

4. *Serious attacks*—incidents of repeated biting and mauling, usually in the neck, face, or throat. These cases required emergency medical attention.

Of the 14 attack cases documented, 4 were considered serious attacks. Two of those occurred in Jasper National Park and one in Yellowstone. Ten minor attacks were documented. Five of those took place in Banff National Park, three in Jasper, and two in Yellowstone. Seven nonattack cases were investigated and fell into the preliminary and persistent categories. Of the seven, five occurred in Jasper National Park and two in Yellowstone.

The table shows the ages of the individuals from each of the categories.

Coyote Attacks on Humans in Western U.S. and Canada 1960–1988*

Age of Victim	Preliminary Category	Persistent Category	Minor Attacks	Serious Attacks
3 and under			1	3
4–8	1		2	1
9–12			1	
13–17	1	1	1	
18 and over	2		5	
Age unknown	2			
Totals	6	1	10	4

*Courtesy of The Wildlife Society.

Here are some details of the four serious attacks, as documented by Carbyn:

1. In the Mammoth area of Yellowstone National Park, November 1960, a 1½-year-old child was moved from a car to a stroller on the porch and left unattended for a short time. A neighbor saw a coyote attacking the child and came to the rescue with a broom. Only after persistent shouting and attacks by three adults did the coyote leave. The child received 21 stitches in the face and had bruises on her back and arms, but was generally protected by a heavy snowsuit.

2. On August 30, 1985, a coyote attacked a four-year-old girl who was playing out of sight, but within hearing distance, of her parents in a Jasper National Park campground. Screaming from the child attracted her parents, who threw rocks at the coyote to scare it off. The child was rushed to the hospital with numerous lacerations on the face.

3. In mid-April 1985 the most serious attack that I investigated occurred in the townsite of Jasper National Park. A mother sent her two-year-old daughter to the backyard to play with a friend. After approximately 10 minutes, the mother went to see the children only to find a coyote dragging the limp body of her child uphill. The coyote's jaws appeared to be clamped around the throat and neck of the child. The coyote dropped the child as her parents rushed toward the animal. The unconscious child was rushed to a nearby hospital with extensive injuries around the face, neck, and throat. However, the child recovered.

4. On July 30, 1988, an 18-month-old girl was walking along a trail at a highway stop with her 10-year-old sister. A coyote attacked the smaller girl, and shortly thereafter the parents arrived. The coyote was biting the neck and head region while the child was lying facedown. As the father picked up the child, the coyote moved back only a few paces. It remained in the area until shot by police within an hour. Rabies tests were negative. Injuries to the child's face, head, and arms were extensive, but generally superficial. More than 200 stitches were required to close the wounds, but there

was no permanent muscle or nerve damage. The incident occurred near Creston, British Columbia.

Carbyn acknowledged that coyotes interact with humans over
large areas of North America; however, he believed that attacks
are rare, or have not been documented in literature. Carbyn
knew of only one case of a human attacked and killed by a coyote—the three-year-old child mentioned previously. The same
coyote also attacked other children. These attacks were linked to
the location of residential districts in mountain canyons with
shrubby vegetation where coyotes frequently visited.

Why do coyotes attack humans? Several reasons might apply.
When Carbyn examined the four most serious attacks on humans, he felt they were predatory in nature. His final discussion
summed it up nicely.

> Coyotes appeared to have lost fear of humans and re-
> garded the children as prey. Loss of fear of humans by
> coyotes has been widespread in national parks and urban
> areas where this predator associates humans with food at
> campgrounds (W. Bradford, Can. Parks Serv., Jasper Natl.
> Park, Alberta, pers. commun.). The process is analogous
> to habituation by bears to food sources associated with
> humans (Herrero 1985, Gilbert 1989).

> Three attacks occurred at times of year when coyotes
> were either about to have pups, or had recently been
> feeding pups. It is significant also that serious attacks
> were made only on infants, the most vulnerable humans.
> It is possible that boldness in coyotes toward humans is
> related to food stress. Coyotes that normally prey on un-
> gulate young may find it more difficult to obtain food as

the season progresses and young ungulates grow larger. Predatory instincts may, therefore, be redirected to other potential sources of food. Having lost the "normal" fear of humans, coyotes may perceive humans as just another potential food item. Till and Knowlton (1983) demonstrated experimentally that predation on domestic sheep can be reduced by destroying pups of depredating adults. It follows that adults with young would be more persistent in their efforts to kill and may therefore be more likely to switch to novel prey if food shortages should occur.

Furthermore, individual coyotes have been known to show unusual behavioral responses to humans. In Riding Mountain National Park, Manitoba, one coyote repeatedly chased cars and snapped at tires (A. Sturko, Can. Parks Serv., Waterton Natl. Park, Alberta, pers. commun.). In the same park, a coyote repeatedly slashed tents in a campground. Similarly, in July 1988, there were several coyote attacks in Banff National Park on campers that were sleeping or resting in sleeping bags (R. J. Haney, Can. Parks Serv., Banff Natl. Park, Alberta, pers. commun.). These events in Banff occurred in the same general area, but it was not possible to determine the number of coyotes involved. It is difficult to determine motivations for tent slashing, tire biting, or sleeping bag "nipping" behavior, and there may not be a common basis for these occurrences.

Carbyn stated that none of the attacks he documented involved rabid coyotes. Instead, he believed that garbage in campgrounds and along highway stopovers likely contributed to the habituation of coyotes to humans.

As mentioned previously in this chapter, the possibility is remote that a coyote will ever attack you. Even if you crawled into a sleeping bag every night next to a drainpipe that harbored a coyote family, you would probably remain safe (I still don't recommend you try this).

Research biologists Bodenchuk, Mason, and Pitt argued that predation management can decrease the risk of attacks and disease transmission from coyotes; thus, management for this purpose should receive strong public support. They added that although the likelihood of a human being attacked or killed by a coyote is low, the annual number of attacks is higher for coyotes than most large animals, such as bears. And although there are no national statistics for coyotes, it has been documented that on average 1.3 people each year in Los Angeles, California, alone are attacked. It's much more common for coyotes to prey upon dogs and cats. Of course, this represents additional loss, and the potential for disease transmission.

Finally, it's the opinion of many specialists that any cost would be justifiable if it meant controlling coyotes that are a threat to human health and safety. After all, millions of dollars have been spent to reduce depredation of livestock. In the preceding chapter I gave precise calculations of costs involved in predation management. In the eyes of many folks, the returns have been worth the effort. Others may disagree. When it comes to human health and safety, though, determining coyote damage costs and control and prevention costs is much more difficult. Nonetheless, who can argue that the cost of predation management isn't worth every penny if it protects human lives?

6

Telltale Sign

QUESTION: How would you stop a coyote from eating watermelons in the garden?

ANSWER: I would get a newspaper and spank him with it.
                    —Erin Cook, age 6

B efore you can even think about outwitting a coyote, or which method you would use to get the job done, you must first determine that Wily is actually responsible for the damage. First, consider that you will seldom catch a coyote in the act. He does much of his dirty work in the dark, and he often makes certain you aren't looking. That's not to say that some coyotes don't mind a little sunshine and the presence of humans; still, most are sneaky about their endeavors and keep you guessing. Consider, too, that other animals may commit the same acts as a coyote.

You may remember the discussion of the DNA testing of a coyote in the previous chapter. A coyote that attacked a human had also bitten into a Frisbee. The Frisbee was taken for analysis to see if it matched the DNA of a coyote that had been trapped near the attack site. Now, most of us won't resort to this identification option when it comes to coyotes attacking prey other than humans, or when they gorge themselves on fruits and garbage. And while DNA testing could determine the precise coyote that caused the damage, most of us will be happy just to know which animal species was responsible.

Predators That Kill

Before getting into the telltale sign of coyotes and other animals, let me first give you an idea of the number of predators out there that commit crimes just like Wily's. By the way, one of these predators you know very well—he could even be your best friend. Yes, dogs are responsible for many of the damages blamed on coyotes. I won't get into "outwitting dogs" in this book, but you should be aware that your best friend could also be a killer.

In 1991 the Agricultural Statistics Board of the USDA reported the estimated number of losses of sheep/lambs and cattle, and the animal species responsible for the predation. The table will show you how important it is to identify the animal causing the damage.

Sheep and Lambs Lost to Coyotes and Dogs*

State	Losses Caused by Coyotes	Losses Caused by Dogs
Alabama	300	200
Alaska	0	2,800
Arizona	5,800	1,335

Sheep and Lambs Lost to Coyotes and Dogs* (Continued)

State	Losses Caused by Coyotes	Losses Caused by Dogs
Arkansas	400	300
California	18,100	6,200
Colorado	32,200	700
Connecticut	0	300
Delaware	0	0
Florida	200	100
Georgia	0	300
Hawaii	0	100
Idaho	8,800	900
Illinois	1,900	1,900
Indiana	300	3,800
Iowa	8,300	5,200
Kansas	2,600	1,000
Kentucky	900	600
Louisiana	400	0
Maine	300	0
Maryland	0	200
Massachusetts	0	0
Michigan	300	700
Minnesota	2,000	900
Mississippi	400	100
Missouri	2,000	1,200
Montana	25,200	1,000
Nebraska	5,700	400
Nevada	9,600	700

(Continued)

Sheep and Lambs Lost to Coyotes and Dogs* (Continued)

State	Losses Caused by Coyotes	Losses Caused by Dogs
New Hampshire	100	200
New Jersey	0	0
New Mexico	14,900	1,400
New York	400	1,000
North Carolina	0	1,900
North Dakota	5,600	1,100
Ohio	1,900	2,500
Oklahoma	7,200	500
Oregon	13,100	8,300
Pennsylvania	0	900
Rhode Island	0	0
South Carolina	0	0
South Dakota	28,900	600
Tennessee	100	400
Texas	56,000	8,000
Utah	21,500	2,100
Vermont	0	0
Virginia	4,100	3,300
Washington	1,300	300
West Virginia	500	1,800
Wisconsin	1,200	300
Wyoming	25,200	1,400

*Estimated number of losses of sheep/lambs, and species of animal that caused the damage, as reported by the Agricultural Statistics Board of the USDA in 1991. Statistics obtained from ADC's Environmental Impact Statement.

Sheep losses caused by other predators, such as bears, foxes, bobcats, and mountain lions, were also listed in the 1991 study. For instance, in Montana (where all predators are present) it was reported that foxes killed an estimated 1,800 sheep, bears killed 700, and bobcats and mountain lions killed 600. Yet by far, coyotes and dogs caused most of the damages.

The number of cattle losses and the species of animal responsible for these losses were also reported in the 1991 study. I won't provide the results for every state, but I will say that coyotes and dogs took top honors. In Alabama an estimated 1,700 cows were lost to coyotes, while dogs brought down 600. In Florida coyotes were responsible for 200 cattle, but dogs brought down 700. The race was close in Kentucky, where coyotes preyed on 1,900 and dogs on 1,500, but not so close in Oklahoma, where coyotes brought down 5,300 and dogs 2,500.

As for poultry, numerous predators may be responsible for doing in your guinea or prized rooster. You may have even seen a coyote in the area, but when you consider that many predators are nocturnal, you can hardly blame Wily for someone else's damage unless you establish proof of the killer. A cat once pulverized a few of my chickens. It wasn't my cat, nor did it belong to anyone else as far as I know. But the cat was tame for the most part and seemed to think that killing the young chickens was the thing to do.

Killers of Poultry

Coyotes
Foxes
Skunks
Raccoons

Feral cats
Dogs
Bobcats
Mother Nature
Minks
Hawks
Owls
Opossums
Weasels
Lynx
Disease
Fellow poultry with attitudes

Killers of Sheep, Goats, Calves, and Foals

Coyotes
Mountain lions
Bobcats
Dogs
Foxes
Mother Nature
Bears
Eagles
Wild pigs
Feral cats
Eagles
Wolves
Lynx

Wolverines
Disease

Killers of Cats and Dogs

Coyotes
Dogs with attitudes
Cats with attitudes
Trucks
Cars
Buses
Bears
Mountain lions
Bobcats
Foxes
Disease
Mother Nature
Furious neighbors

You should also be realistic if you find your pet dog or cat lying dead in the bushes. He might look as though a coyote mangled him, but someone else's pet may have attacked yours. On the other hand, it could be that your pet was hit by a vehicle and ran or crawled a considerable distance from the road before succumbing. You simply shouldn't take for granted that a coyote killed your pet (although he might have wished he had).

Telltale Tracks and Scat

Before blaming a coyote for killing, you must first know that the missing animal, or animals, are dead. When it comes to livestock, vultures are sometimes spotted hovering over a dead animal, or on the ground feeding on a dead animal. If the animal has been shredded by scavenging birds, it becomes more difficult to determine the cause of death.

Wily may outthink and outsmart his prey, and he may do it when we least suspect it, but he cannot always avoid leaving telltale sign. He may leave tracks, scat, or both—either are distinguishable from other animals' sign—and he'll probably kill his prey using a recognizable method. Sometimes the killing sign varies depending upon the struggle of his victim, the experience of the coyote, the size of the animal he attacks, and in some cases the personality of the coyote. However, if you're able to locate his prey after the attack, and after Wily has left the scene, an examination of the area may leave little or no doubt that the attacker was a coyote.

Although coyote scat resembles dog scat, there are a few distinct differences. Coyote scat is somewhat twisted, whereas the scat of a dog is not. More than likely, the coyote scat will contain hair easily visible to the eye. For those who get a kick out of examining coyote scat closely, it's even possible to find feathers and bone fragments. Dog scat may contain hair if the animal has recently fed upon another animal, but scat completely laced with hair is probably that of a coyote. Coyote scat is usually smaller than dog scat. Normally, the diameter of coyote scat could be compared to the diameter of a cigar. Coyote scat is usually dark gray, but might appear somewhat pink if the animal has fed on watermelons. Dog droppings are usually brown.

Coyotes prefer to defecate along trails. This may be a logging road, or even a trail used by humans. Occasionally, they will defecate on rock piles. However, when a coyote spends time feeding on prey or carrion, it may also defecate nearby.

You probably have a better chance of finding coyote tracks than scat, even if the coyote has spent a lot of time near a kill site. However, sandy or moist soil is a requirement. Even a coyote that weighs more than 30 pounds won't leave tracks unless soft soil is present.

All members of the Canidae family have similar tracks. That goes for coyotes, foxes, wolves, and dogs. Wolf and dog tracks are more similar to each other than coyote and fox tracks. All of the Canidae have four toes. There are five digits, including the dewclaw.

Just so you don't confuse the tracks of a member of the Felidae family (cat) with those of a coyote, I'll explain the major difference. Cats have retractable claws. Thus, you usually won't see claw marks in their tracks (exceptions exist in snow and sandy soil). That goes for tracks of bobcats, lynx, domesticated cats, and mountain lions.

The track of a coyote is somewhat oblong (longer than it is wide) and not as rounded as that of a dog or wolf. Coyote tracks are also smaller than the tracks of a dog or wolf. A wolf track may be up to 5 inches long, and a track of a large dog 4 or 4½ inches. The coyote track is seldom more than 3 inches long, although the hind feet are about ½ inch shorter than the front feet. The claw marks are visible in coyotes, dogs, and wolves, but are more distinct in dogs and wolves. Another noticeable differ-

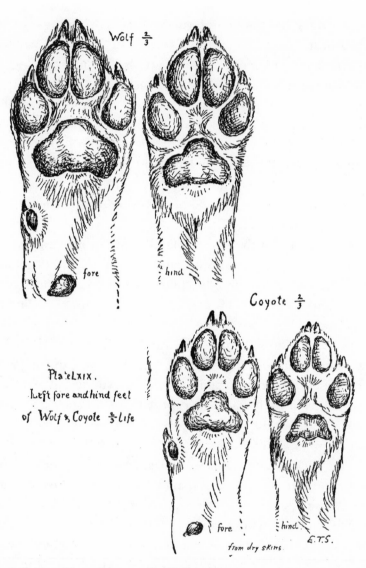

Wolf ⅔

fore   hind

Coyote ⅔

PlateLxix.
Left fore and hind feet
of Wolf & Coyote ⅔-Life

fore   hind

from dry skins   E.T.S.

The distinct paw of the coyote leaves an identifiable track.

ence between dog and coyote tracks is the pattern. Coyotes usually walk straighter lines than dogs. Dog tracks seem to zigzag and seldom travel far in a straight line.

There are a couple of noticeable differences between coyote and fox tracks. The track of a gray fox is seldom more than 1½ inches long. Red fox tracks are seldom more than 2 inches long. Fox tracks are also more rounded than the coyote's oblong track. When a coyote walks, each track will be spaced about 12 inches apart, compared to about 8 inches apart for the fox. Because of numerous hairs on the feet of a fox, the track is seldom as distinct as that of a coyote.

Scavenging or Predation

When it comes to livestock and poultry deaths, and sometimes the death of a pet, there are factors to consider other than predation. Parasites and disease cause some animal deaths. Rarely, an animal eats a poisonous plant. In some cases, cold temperatures or lightning causes death. Once the animal dies, it may attract scavengers, such as coyotes, ravens, crows, or opossums, that may be seen feeding on the carcass.

Sometimes coyote scat and tracks are found near a dead animal. Almost immediately, most folks will charge Wily with first-degree murder and prepare to pass sentence. If they see a coyote run away from a carcass, they will surely point the finger at you-know-who. Nevertheless, as I have said before, a coyote is as much a scavenger as he is a predator. But even with this in mind, don't assume that a coyote is *not* responsible for killing the animal you just found.

To determine if predation was a factor, always approach the animal cautiously, taking care to preserve valuable evidence. If you spot blood, avoid walking over it. Make certain you don't move the carcass until you've examined it as necessary.

Inspect the animal and the area surrounding the carcass. A great deal of blood is a sure sign of predation, particularly in the hide near the location of a wound. Profuse bleeding is a result of an animal attacked while the heart is still pumping. Some bleeding occurs after death, but this lasts only for moments. If the animal died of causes other than predation, more than likely signs of severe hemorrhaging would not be present unless another form of traumatic death occurred.

When a predator kills an animal, his prey is usually found lying on its side. If it died of other causes, it could be lying with its legs tucked under its body. Also, check to see if the animal was dragged. It could have been killed in one location but taken to another. Some predators practice this technique. If debris is present on the ground, you'll see a flattened area where the animal once lay. This is another good location to look for blood to determine if hemorrhaging occurred.

You probably won't want to skin the dead animal you find (particularly if it's a beloved pet), but this is another method you can use to find out if predation occurred and, for that matter, get some indication of which predator killed the animal. When coyotes attack, they usually bite the animal along the neck and throat. This is the method used by most solitary coyotes, but sometimes a pack will attack the legs and hips of their prey. When a predator bites the animal, even if it's not a severe bite, hemorrhaging will occur under the skin. The same thing happens, though, when a predatory bird attacks an animal. The hemorrhaged area soon becomes a bruise.

If the animal in question doesn't have a thick hide, you can try skinning a small portion of the hide surrounding what appears to be the wound. This is the only way to observe bruising. If the animal has a thick hide, as do sheep, you may need to skin the animal's entire neck to look for bruises. Once the animal is skinned, you should also look for bite marks.

Inspect the area surrounding the dead animal, taking notice of broken tree limbs, leaves, and other debris that might have moved around. Also check for bare ground in areas that weren't barren previously. When a coyote preys upon an animal, particularly a large animal, there's usually a struggle that's certain to disturb the surroundings. If a scavenger wasn't responsible for killing the animal and only fed on it, there will be little or no disturbance to the area, except where it may have lain down while feeding.

Sometimes livestock producers find newborn lambs, kids, or calves that have been scavenged upon. They don't know if predation occurred or if the animal was stillborn. Livestock are often stillborn, which sets the stage for scavenging. Then again, it's quite common for a predator, such as a coyote, to attack and kill newborn livestock within minutes or seconds of them taking their first breaths.

Believe it or not, there are a couple of things you can do to determine if predation occurred or if the animal was stillborn—if you don't mind getting into the carcass of the dead animal. First, you can cut the animal along the underneath side of its abdomen, making certain you don't push the knife blade in too deeply. This could puncture an organ before you have the chance to examine it. Once you have access to the organs, find the stomach and look inside for milk. Most mammals suck milk minutes after birth. If milk is present, the animal wasn't stillborn.

You can also inspect the lungs of the animal, but, again, make certain you don't puncture them. If they appear pink, feel spongy, and are lightweight, rest assured that the animal was born alive. If the lungs are purple or dark red and feel heavy, the animal didn't breathe and was stillborn. If you have any doubts as to the color of the lungs and their weight, place them in a bucket of water. If the animal breathed, the lungs will float. If the lungs sink, the animal was stillborn.

Sheep raisers can also inspect the hooves of lambs. Soft tissue covers the sole of the hoof when the animal is born. If the animal got to its feet and moved around for a few minutes, the tissue will have worn off.

You should also inspect the newborn's umbilical cord. Although the mother will often clean the exposed end of the cord, a close examination may tell you if the animal was alive when born. A stillborn animal won't have a distinct blood clot on the exposed end of the umbilical cord, whereas you will see a clot on one that was alive at birth.

The more time that elapses between the death of the animal and your inspection, the more difficult it will be to determine if predation occurred. Just how much time you have to make an accurate determination depends upon when the scavenging began, how many animals were scavenging, and weather conditions that could have accelerated decomposition.

Determining if predation occurred isn't always easy. However, a patient and persistent individual without any type of wildlife damage experience can usually tell ·if predation, scavenging, or both has occurred. It's simply a matter of putting the puzzle together, one piece at a time. Sometimes you'll fail to determine if predation occurred. It may be due to weather, the season, and how much time passed before you found the animal in question. And yes, even experts have had difficulty trying to solve the puzzle. Nevertheless, once you do solve it, you have another task ahead. A much more difficult and larger puzzle to solve: Which predator killed the animal?

Is Wily to Blame?

Okay, you've resolved the matter. You're pretty doggoned sure that predation occurred. Now it's time to determine "who" is responsible. You are sad, angered, discouraged, bewildered, and frustrated. Your bank account also may have shrunk a little. You want revenge and you don't want the same thing to happen again. Before exacting revenge and gaining satisfaction by reading the remainder of this book, however, you must determine if Wily was the predator responsible for the act.

Fortunately, many biologists and other wildlife specialists have observed and documented predators in action, and have made close inspections of prey following the attack to determine predation patterns. Yet, before I pass along the extensive killing patterns of several species, including the coyote, I want to refer back to dogs and coyotes for just a moment. I've already told you that dogs kill almost as many mammals as coyotes; therefore, I have summarized a few of their livestock killing patterns below. I suggest you study these before moving onto the detailed predation patterns of livestock, poultry, and pets in the pages that follow.

Telltale Sign

Coyote	Dog
Usually attack front of victim	Usually attack rear of victim
Bite marks found on throat of victim	Bite marks found everywhere on victim
Seldom chews on ears and tails of victim	Often chews on ears and tails of victim
Usually kills one animal each day	Often kills more than one animal each day
May drag the remains of victim away	Seldom drags the remains of victim away
Other nearby animals slightly stressed	Other nearby animals severely stressed
Feeds upon the animal it attacks	Seldom feeds upon the animal it attacks

Now that you have seen the primary facts, I'll get even more serious. The predation patterns that follow are not what you want to read to your child at bedtime, but they sure will help you when predation occurs. So you might as well grab a little coffee, take two aspirins, and start reading.

Predation Patterns

Coyotes

Most animals killed by coyotes will have bite marks under the neck in the throat area. Foamy blood in the area of the windpipe may be observed, as well as a broken jaw. It's also common for a coyote to bite the animal's nose, particularly when he preys upon cattle and larger game animals. The larger the coyote's prey, and the less experience the coyote has at killing, the more likely you are to find bites to the hindquarters and legs. If pups are involved in the kill (usually in summer), bites may be found on the legs of the animal. However, most coyote attacks don't last long. They usually bring their prey down for keeps quickly unless it's a large animal. They sometimes do begin feeding, though, before the animal is dead. If you find more than one dead animal, or find additional animals injured, dogs may be responsible for the killings. Coyotes are usually satisfied with one kill, except when pups are young and in the process of learning how to bring down prey. Coyote attacks on livestock occur most frequently near fringes of fields where cover exists.

Coyotes are usually satisfied with one kill—except when they are feeding pups.

The cover provides a hiding place if a quick escape is necessary. Rarely, coyotes will begin feeding on the hindquarters. Most will begin feeding at the last rib, pulling out the entrails first. Their preferences are the liver, heart, lungs, and kidneys; they seldom eat the stomach or intestines, unless the stomach contains milk. Once the preferred organs are consumed, coyotes begin feeding on bones and the meaty portions of their prey. Bone fragments may be found where the coyote had lain and ate. Unlike dogs—which usually don't come back to a kill to feed later—a coyote will usually continue to scavenge on the animal, sometimes for several days. When coyotes attack poultry and small pets, they often leave little or no sign. In most cases, they carry their victim to another location, unless blocked by a fence. If poultry or a pet comes up missing and fencing surrounds the area, look for remains of the victim along the fence. Since a coyote seldom feeds upon dogs, you may locate a carcass near the attack site. A coyote might attack a dog that gets close to the den and pups, but probably won't feed it to the pups unless no other foods are available.

Dogs

Most dogs will attack in the daylight hours, whereas a coyote will most likely attack at night or during early morning or late afternoon. When a dog attacks an animal, he doesn't begin with the neck and throat. He usually bites the animal in several locations. For this reason, the predation of a mutilated animal is often blamed on a dog. Another reason for mutilation is that a dog, or dogs, will take longer to bring down an animal than does a coyote. Unlike coyotes, which often bring down the youngest of livestock animals, dogs are not selective and will attack adults. Pay close attention to see if other members of the flock that weren't preyed upon are stressed. Dogs tend to stress animals during an attack. The quicker kill of a coyote does not stress the other animals as much; some will even stand back and watch while their buddy takes it on the nose (I mean that literally). When dogs attack livestock, other animals in the herd may run and pant excessively. After a dog kills his prey, he may begin running another animal immediately, whereas a coyote will probably be satisfied to feed on one kill and leave the other animals alone. When dogs attack livestock such as sheep, you may find two or more carcasses in open areas away from cover. If you locate the dead prey soon after the kill, you'll probably notice confusion and nervousness among the herd. Dogs are much messier than coyotes when it comes to killing. When dogs kill sheep, it's common to find clumps of wool in several locations. When they kill cattle, you may see pieces of hide lying on the ground. When they kill poultry, you could find feathers strewn over a large area. Although dogs seldom feed on their prey, one exception is feral dogs that survive in the wild. Nevertheless, most dogs enjoy killing much more than eating. When they do feed upon their kill, they usually begin at the anus. In other words, they start from the outside and work in, whereas a coyote most often begins inside and works outward.

Wolves

Wolves often prey upon cattle and sheep, and sometimes on horses. Unlike coyotes, they might attack large cattle when calves are not available. When wolves attack livestock, they begin with a chase, savagely biting at the hindquarters and back legs of the animal. These wounds are easily noticed unless wolves have eaten a major portion of the victim before you arrive. Bites on the shoulders and front legs may also be observed. Neck and throat bites are less common, but do occur when wolves attack large livestock. Once their prey falls, wolves will begin tearing the guts out of the animal, and will usually begin feeding on its hindquarters. Typically, bone fragments will be seen in the area surrounding the prey. After the initial feeding, the wolf will leave a large animal and return to feed again later. Small livestock animals, if not eaten in their entirety during the first feeding, may be dragged to another location a short distance away. Since coyote and wolf attacks are similar when both go for the throat of their victim, the bite marks should be examined. During the kill, a coyote often must adjust his clamp on the throat, whereas a wolf will usually hold the animal in a single location. Wolf scat may be found near the carcass and will contain hair and bone like that of a coyote, but wolf scat is larger.

Bears

When a bear attacks another animal, it doesn't rely on suffocation to the throat, as does a coyote. Instead, it prefers to use its strength to crush the skull, the neck vertebrae, or the spine. In some cases, shock kills its prey. Because of the bear's long claws, it's also common to find claw marks on the body of the animal. Sometimes a bear will straddle its victim. The larger the animal it attacks, the better the chance of finding claw marks along the back and sides of the animal. The bite marks of a black bear are

A close examination soon after a kill may reveal "whodunit." Many times, a coyote takes the blame for another predator, such as a black bear.

usually spaced 3½ to 4½ inches apart. Like dogs, but often unlike coyotes, a bear may prey upon more than one animal during a killing episode. It's also common for a bear to partially skin its prey as it begins feeding. The hide will not be mutilated and torn, except for visible scratch marks. Since a bear prefers meat, it usually begins feeding on the hams of the animal. Rarely does it feed on entrails, except for the liver, heart, lungs, and kidneys. A bear may eat the entire carcass of a small animal over time, but when it kills a large animal, it'll eat what it can and save the rest for later. A bear usually drags the carcass into brush after the kill. Black bears seldom cover the carcass with weeds and dirt, but grizzly bears often do so to hide their prey from scavengers.

Mountain Lions

As will bears, mountain lions often attack the neck and back of their prey. They often kill by inducing a massive hemorrhage. Large claw marks are visible on the head and neck, and sometimes on the back and shoulders. The tooth punctures of the upper canines will be 1¾ to 2¼ inches apart, and the lower canines about 1¼ to 1¾ inches apart. A mountain lion will tend to dismantle the carcass a piece at a time, but it seldom feeds upon the stomach and intestines; it usually moves these organs aside, sometimes a few feet from the kill. Lions eat the hams first, but will feed upon the rest of the remaining portion of the carcass. When they kill a larger animal, they'll drag it away and cover it after feeding for a short time.

Bobcats

A bobcat won't hesitate to jump on the back of a large animal to bring it down. When it attacks smaller animals, it usually grabs the throat and neck of the animal while standing on all fours, similar to the method used by the cats of Africa. Claw marks may be found along the neck and back of the prey, and claw punctures and severe hemorrhage might be seen on the neck. Bite marks are about ¾ inch apart. They're also easier to find and measure than the bite marks of foxes and coyotes, because bobcats don't bite their victim repeatedly. However, sometimes a bobcat kill is difficult to distinguish from a coyote kill. The tracks of a bobcat are about 2 to 3 inches in diameter. Bobcats also begin feeding on the animal behind the last rib, savoring the taste of the liver, heart, and lungs, but they're more likely than coyotes are to eat the stomach and intestines. Bobcats often drag away their kill and cover it to protect it from scavengers.

Eagles

Bald eagles don't kill livestock as often as golden eagles, but both will scavenge on carrion. Golden eagles have also been observed killing deer and antelope. It's common to find punctures in an animal's body after an eagle attack. These puncture marks come primarily from the bird's middle claws (eagles have three claws on the front and one claw on the back of both feet). The punctures will be anywhere from 1 to 3 inches apart. Claw punctures are deeper than the marks of a canine's teeth. Severe internal hemorrhages may also occur at the puncture wound, but signs of this might not be visible, because the eagle will feed on the bloody areas. Keep in mind that other scavenging birds, such as ravens and buzzards, may leave round puncture holes that look like claw marks on the attacked animal's head. Typically, scavenging birds will peck the victim's head. You may also find strips of hide, because an eagle skins its prey inside out. This is particularly noticeable in the hide near the ribs. Further, the neck and legs of the eagle's prey will remain attached, whereas they are dismantled by some predators, such as bears. Although many predators don't feed on the entrails, an eagle does enjoy the internal organs, although rarely does it eat the stomach. Occasionally, it will crush the skull and feed on the brain. The eagle's white-streaked feces are occasionally found near the prey.

Hawks and Owls

Goshawks, red-tailed hawks, and great horned owls are common predators of chickens, ducks, guineas, and game birds. Sometimes it's difficult to determine which raptor killed a bird, but one of the best methods of identification is to pay close attention to the sky above you and the trees around you. Many raptors used to people will remain there, waiting for an opportunity to strike again; however, hawks and owls usually kill only one bird each day. Raccoons, skunks, and other predators may kill several birds at a time, but rarely will hawks and owls. When owls kill, they usually bite off and eat the head of the bird. An obvious sign of hawk predation is a pile of feathers near the carcass. Hawks usually pluck away the feathers neatly. Owls also pluck away feathers, but they sometimes swallow small birds whole. Hawks and owls are also capable of clutching small chickens and ducks and flying away with them. Owls may swallow bone, which could be found in their droppings. Hawks seldom swallow bones.

Domestic Cats

Whether they are house cats kept as family pets or feral strays that have been abandoned in the wild, domestic cats can influence the balance of wild predators (for instance, coyotes, foxes, raccoons, or bobcats) and their prey. The attack methods of feral and house cats are much like those of bobcats, although house cats are more apt to kill for sport than for food. Thus, after killing its prey, a house cat may eat none or only a portion of it. Sometimes feral cats attack lambs, but both feral cats and house cats will kill poultry and other birds. A Wisconsin study indicated that 35 percent of a rural cat's annual diet is songbirds. When either kind of domestic cat attacks poultry, it often grabs it at the neck with its teeth while holding it in multiple places; the entire neck may be free of feathers when it's found. The cat's claws, which grip the bird, will also rip the feathers from its back. Tracks may be found at the kill scene and are usually about 2 to 2½ inches in diameter, but since cats usually bury their scat, it's unlikely that any will be found near the attack site.

Raccoons

When a raccoon attacks poultry, it usually rips the head away from the neck. Sometimes the head is found a few feet away from the carcass. Raccoons prefer to feed on the breast of poultry but occasionally eat the crop. They also eat the eggs of poultry if available. If you find poultry alive with a leg or foot missing, it could have been attacked by a raccoon, but managed to escape. Occasionally, raccoons will attack dogs and cats, particularly if the pet threatens them. This usually turns out to be a big mistake for the pet. When a raccoon attacks a pet, it often bites into the back of its neck until it kills it. Raccoons have even attacked large dogs by climbing onto the back and riding the dog like a jockey on a horse. However, they probably won't eat your pet. The raccoon's tracks are unmistakable. They have five toes on their handlike front feet.

Foxes

Both red and gray foxes attack poultry and sometimes small pets. They commonly attack at the throat. In some cases the back of their prey will be riddled with bite and scratch marks. If the victim is a small animal, such as a chicken, duck, or cat, the fox usually carries it away to its den to begin feeding. When foxes attack large birds, such as turkeys, they'll leave a much bigger mess at the kill site than will a coyote. Since a fox is smaller than a coyote, it will have a more difficult time trying to bring down his victim. When one kills a large bird, you'll also find numerous feathers scattered about, left behind after the bird struggled to get away but was attacked repeatedly by the persistent fox. Like the coyote, the fox begins feeding behind the ribs, and sometimes it will eat the flanks. Occasionally, it will eat the tongue and nose of an animal. Bone fragments are seldom found, because the fox rarely chews on them. It may pull portions out of the animal and bury them to feed on later. The bite marks of a fox are smaller than those of a coyote. The upper canines will be spaced only ½ to ¾ inch apart.

Skunks, Minks, and Weasels

Although skunks cause far more problems digging and holing up near homes and outbuildings, they do occasionally kill poultry; however, they don't climb over fences as readily as other predators, such as raccoons, weasels, and minks. Skunks probably prefer eggs to fowl, but they won't hesitate to kill fowl when opportunity allows. Skunks don't mutilate poultry as violently as some predators will, such as raccoons and dogs. They usually bite the neck and head when they attack, and numerous feathers may also be plucked. Minks and weasels also bite the neck and head of poultry, but neither will usually drag away the victim. In most cases, minks and weasels will make an even smaller mess when killing poultry than would a skunk. Minks and weasels may kill several birds at a time. They usually pile the birds up, but eat only one before leaving the area. Rarely, a mink may attack a small pet. After killing the animal, he neatly skins the animal inside out as he feeds.

Coyotes and Melons

Coyotes eat all melons but dearly love watermelons. Many folks in southern states, portions of the Midwest, and California have suffered major losses of melon crops due to coyote damage.

There's not much you can say about recognizing telltale sign of a coyote in a melon patch, except that tracks and scat may be found if the ground is sandy and clean of debris. You can also look at the bite marks in the rind of the melon. The upper canines of a coyote (the first to sink into a melon rind) are about 1⅜ inches apart. The lower canines are about 1⅛ to 1¼ inches apart. If you find bite marks in the rind anywhere between 1⅛ and 1⅜ inches apart, a coyote could be responsible for the damage. Other animals with similar spacing between the canines could also be responsible, however. As for overall destruction of a melon, it may vary. A coyote may obliterate one melon, but bite another in only two or three locations.

Raccoons also eat watermelons, but their telltale sign is a single hole in the melon. Once they make the hole, they will pull out the contents through it with their front feet until they finish feeding.

Unusual Telltale Sign

A coyote may exhibit unusual symptoms or behavior when illness or injuries occur. Humans sometimes observe this. The good news is that if you can detect such strange sign before damage has occurred, or a short time after, you can implement actions to prevent further damage to pets and human safety.

If you notice a coyote that seems to love walking in and out of buildings, you have a problem coyote. Once a coyote has lost a fear of entering dwellings, be they barns or garages where human scent is abundantly spread about, you can bet your pretty little kitty that he's up to no good. In the previous chapter I told the story of a coyote that entered a house and attempted to drag away a child.

Moreover, how about a coyote that walks around attacking things that don't breathe? Yep, that has happened too. Coyotes have chased cars and bit at tires. Crazy, but true. They have also been observed stalking and attacking lots of nonliving things that don't move. These things don't have to resemble a puppy dog or Mary's Little Lamb. Who knows why a coyote would stalk and attack a two-foot-tall concrete statue of a frog taking up space in the middle of a flower garden? But it's happened. Obviously, any coyote that reacts this way is probably going to be a pest before long, or has already become one.

You may also see a coyote that acts sickly. He may stagger around and appear to be partially paralyzed. He may even bite at himself furiously. All of these behaviors are symptoms of disease. Any coyote that exhibits this behavior should be reported to the authorities in your area immediately.

Each species has its unique sign.

If a coyote is responsible for the various types of damages mentioned in this chapter, the time has come to consider a method of control. A problem coyote rarely commits one crime and quits. Of course, maybe I shouldn't say that Wily has "committed a crime." In most cases of predation, a coyote is simply doing what comes naturally. Nonetheless, when his acts threaten human health and safety, or result in damage to property, it's sometimes sad and often costly. That's when you must outwit him.

7

Control Alternatives

QUESTION: *How would you stop a coyote from eating watermelons in the garden?*

ANSWER: *I would stop growing watermelons and grow tomatoes instead.*
—Allyson Harlowe, age 12

Okay, you've finally determined a coyote is responsible for damages. The process might have taken an hour, a week, or six months, but now you know. It's also now that you must decide how you will deal with the predator. Once you make this decision, it may take an hour, a week, or six months to accomplish the task. In fact, you might never resolve the matter. Putting an end to the bad habits of a shrewd coyote is often an overwhelming challenge. Try to end the bad habits of three shrewd coyotes and it could become an impossible task. One thing is certain, however: If you choose to do nothing at all to stop Wily and his cohorts, your problems will not go away.

Every control alternative is dependent upon the type of damage caused by the coyote. There are many methods, all of which will be discussed in later chapters. What you must do first is decide whether eradication is best. In other words, do you pass the death sentence, or should you consider a nonlethal method of control? These are your two alternatives.

Before continuing, let me first say that if a coyote becomes a threat to human health and safety, there's no debate. A lethal method of control is the only appropriate option. It doesn't really matter if it isn't the coyote's fault, either. I don't know of any officials who would give a coyote a second chance once he poses a threat to humans.

A decision to kill, or not to kill, might very well depend upon the type of damage the coyote causes. It may also depend upon the possibility of future damage. Thus, you might want to begin the control procedure with a nonlethal method, subject to change to lethal without notice. You should also consider the possibility that more than one coyote is causing the damage. It could be a pack of coyotes, or it could be a mating pair. Legality is another issue. If you think it best to kill the coyote, make certain the method you choose is legal in the area where you'll do the killing. If not, you must choose a nonlethal control method, or consider turning the problem over to someone else (that's not always possible, but will be discussed in more detail in chapter 12).

The legal status of coyotes varies depending on state and provincial laws. It may even come down to their classification—predator or furbearing game animal. In most western states coyotes are classified as predators and can be taken throughout the entire year. It doesn't matter whether they're causing damage to livestock. In other areas a closed season may be specified. Coyotes may be protected year-round, or during a few months of the year. In some cases, coyotes may be killed only during a designated season, and sometimes only by specific methods. Here are the possibilities you must consider before killing coyotes:

- If you want to kill a problem coyote, you might be able to get state or federal assistance.
- It may or may not be legal to shoot coyotes throughout the year.
- It may or may not be legal to hunt coyotes at night.
- It may or may not be lawful to hunt coyotes with an electronic game-calling device.
- It may or may not be lawful to hunt coyotes over bait.
- Your choice of weapons may be limited.
- Traps and/or snares may or may not be legal.
- Under certain circumstances, you may be given permission to kill protected coyotes.
- Laws governing the killing of coyotes may not be uniform throughout a state or province.
- A landowner or livestock owner may have more rights than others to eradicate coyotes.
- Laws governing the killing of coyotes are subject to change at a moment's notice.

My questionnaire asked each state and province if it classified the coyote as a game animal, and whether a closed season existed. I didn't obtain answers from every state and province, and a few of the answers were a little sketchy. For instance, some were reluctant to say that the coyote is a "game animal." Some say he's a "furbearing animal," while others simply list him as a predator. Nevertheless, I'll pass along some of this information to you.

Pennsylvania considers the coyote a game animal. A closed season is designated for trapping coyotes, but licensed hunters may take coyotes all year. The trapping season usually begins in mid-October and continues through mid-February. New Brunswick classifies the coyote as a game animal, but also considers him a varmint; thus, he's not protected by game laws and can be taken anytime except during the three-day moose-hunting season. Wisconsin also considers the coyote a game animal, but allows landowners to shoot or trap coyotes anytime on their property. Wisconsin hunters can shoot coyotes all year, but trappers have a designated season. In Michigan coyotes are considered game animals. They can be hunted anytime except April 16 through July 14, although property owners can hunt or trap coyotes on their property at any time of the year if animals are causing property damage.

As do some other states and provinces, Maine allows year-round hunting, but trapping is seasonal. Maine classifies the coyote as a game animal. South Carolina says it doesn't classify the coyote as a game animal, except when he's hunted. There's no closed season, and hunters can use electronic calls during daylight hours only. In Florida the coyote is not considered a game animal and he can be live-trapped, hunted with dogs, and taken with snares or firearms year-round. You will need a special permit from the executive director of the Florida Fish and Wildlife Commission, though, to use a padded-jaw steel trap.

Some states classify the coyote as a game animal, or furbearing animal, but have no closed season, which means you can hunt them year-round. These include Kentucky, Ohio, Rhode Island, South Dakota, and Illinois (except during portions of the firearm deer hunting season). Some states and provinces also classify the coyote as a game animal, or furbearing animal, but have a closed season, which means you can hunt them only during specific times of the year. These include Alaska, New York, Massachusetts, New Jersey, Nova Scotia, and Indiana.

Many states and provinces classify the coyote as a predator. Their wildlife departments don't protect coyotes, and they allow hunting all year. The list includes Arizona, California, Delaware, Georgia, Idaho, Kansas, Oklahoma, Minnesota, Montana, Nebraska, Oregon, Utah, Washington, West Virginia, and Wyoming.

Every state and provincial department seems to have its own ideas about managing coyotes. Most of them do consider this predator a vital link in the ecosystem, and a link that's necessary to its future. Nevertheless, if the truth were known, there are probably fewer management options for coyotes than for some game animals. It's also true that department officials probably find it more difficult to manage coyotes than some game animals. Has any department ever set management goals that would *increase* its coyote population? I seriously doubt it. In fact, such goals are usually specifically designed to reduce the population. Many of these have failed, however.

Shooting and trapping coyotes are lethal measures you can consider, providing local regulations allow these measures. I'll discuss both these techniques in upcoming chapters.

You should also know that eradication is not always the answer. If only one coyote is causing your problem, his death might put an end to damages—at least temporarily. Yet often another coyote will move into the previous coyote's territory a short time after the removal of the problem animal. On a larger scale, if it's a pack of coyotes doing damage, you could remove several of them and shortly after have several *more* move into the area. Coyotes are territorial. If residents are removed, others usually waste little time claiming the available turf. There's also the question of ecological balance. If too many coyotes are removed is it possible that their prey, such as rodents, would then overpopulate and cause additional problems?

With the goal to answer questions such as these, Scott E. Henke and Fred C. Bryant of the Department of Range and Wildlife Management at Texas Tech University conducted a study of predator-prey interactions on four sites at the University of Texas lands in Andrews and Martin counties. On two of the sites, designated "treatment sites," aerial gunning was used to eliminate 354 coyotes from April 1990 to January 1992. The other two sites were left alone to allow predators to predate normally. Coyotes were the most abundant predator in the areas, but other predators also found in them included badgers, bobcats, striped skunks, and gray foxes. A variety of rodents, including kangaroo rats, black-tailed jackrabbits, and desert cottontail rabbits were the coyote's primary prey in the two sites.

Now, you probably don't give a hoot about kangaroo rats, but you should know that they quickly became the most abundant rodent species on the sites where coyotes had been removed. Keep in mind that not all of the coyote population was eliminated on the treatment sites. Officials estimated that 50 percent of the coyotes were removed. Nonetheless, kangaroo rats ranked pretty far up on the coyote's food list, and when half of the coyotes had been removed, kangaroo rat populations proliferated considerably.

After the removal, Henke and Bryant noted that the kangaroo rat dominated rodent communities in both grassland and shrubland habitat. Of course, we could assume this was bad news for other rodents. "As the population of kangaroo rats increased, so did the level of interspecific competition, thus reducing rodent species richness," Henke and Bryant observed.

Anytime there is a population increase of a particular animal, such as the kangaroo rat, the lifestyles of other animals may also be affected. Consider when coyotes were removed— that caused the increase in rats. They began infesting habitats once favored by other animals. The normal preying pattern of other predators was also disturbed. It's a chain reaction.

Jackrabbits also proliferated in the treatment site areas. Their increase may also affect nature's balance. An increased population of jackrabbits often results in an overuse of vegetation. This might seem like a minor problem to some, but it's rough on those who own livestock in the same area. The bottom line: Jackrabbits and livestock compete for food.

Nonetheless, ranchers don't believe that coyote control has a great impact on the balance of ecosystems. They say coyotes are resilient, responding to control efforts with greater litter sizes (biologists have proven this to be true). Therefore, coyote removal could never reach eradication levels that would affect the ecosystem.

It is a fact that a drop in a coyote population often leads to younger females breeding, and we also know that litter sizes increase. These are nature's ways of making certain that predators remain. Nevertheless, in some cases greater damage may be incurred by livestock owners if too many coyotes are eradicated, and particularly when alpha males and females are removed. If you remove a mating pair of coyotes before their pups are weaned, you can safely assume that the pups won't see their first birthday. On the other hand, if the mating pair is eradicated after the pups have left the den but before the pups are on their own, livestock predation may only increase. The pups didn't complete their hunting education, so they may have problems hunting and killing wild animals, finding it expedient to prey upon easier animals such as livestock. As for litter sizes increasing, you can also assume that the bigger the litter, the more mouths there are to feed. That means a breeding pair of coyotes may find it necessary to kill more livestock. Coyotes are often removed from ecosystems because of their predatory nature; however, wildlife and livestock managers need to realize that trade-offs exist concerning coyote control.

Varying durations of coyote control may produce varying results. Henke, in his article "Effects of Coyote Control on Their Prey: A Review," said that results of studies of ecosystem changes due to coyote removal often appear ambiguous because of this variability. Short-term coyote removal efforts (six months or less) typically haven't resulted in increases in the prey base, but long-term, intensive coyote removal reportedly has altered the species composition within the ecosystem.

Henke also noted the disparate views of ranchers, wildlife biologists, environmentalists, and urbanites on the role of coyotes in ecosystems. Historically, livestock managers have been the group most concerned with coyotes, because of depredation. Today, many other folks are equally concerned. There are people who lose exotic animals to coyotes. There are individuals in the rural areas and suburbs who lose poultry to coyotes. There are also the urban folks who have experienced a wide array of coyote problems.

Most would agree that the Wildlife Services (WS) facility at Utah State University is the leading predator research complex in the world. Scientists assigned to the facility are committed to research support of the WS operational program and the development of alternative methods of predator damage management. Past contributions of the Logan, Utah, field station include the collection of data that:

- documented that coyotes are abundant and that predator control has negligible effects on populations;
- demonstrated that denning is a selective depredation control method and defended denning against judicial challenges;
- supported aerial gunning in winter on high mountain grazing allotments—coyotes present in winter are also present the following summer;
- showed that coyotes without pups tend not to kill large prey like livestock and some game animals, such as antelope;
- pioneered the use of tranquilizer trap devices (TTDs) for capturing coyotes, and validated coyote attractants and repellents.

Russ Mason, a dedicated scientist at the Logan field station, said the wild canid facility there is the largest in the country, if not the world. At all times, a team of scientists is working with 125 to 175 coyotes in settings ranging from kennels to 20-acre pastures. They're currently testing guard animals, selective attractants, and the use of reproductive inhibition as ways of managing depredating behavior, as well as studying interactions between coyotes and other canids, such as some species of foxes. They're also nearing completion of the analysis and publication of a three-year data set on coyote behavior and ecology from Yellowstone National Park.

If I had to guess, I'd say that controlling coyotes with non-lethal methods is preferable to most folks than lethal methods. Today, there's a growing concern for animal welfare in North America. That's not to say I'm taking a stand on nonlethal methods of control. On the contrary, I've already been involved in the eradication of coyotes when deemed necessary. I've also spared a few that I could have done away with.

If you're thinking of offering a bounty for the removal of problem coyotes, you could be on the right track but probably don't have a full understanding of how a bounty system works. If you're hoping that your state or province will enact a bounty system for coyotes, you're on the wrong train. Many individuals do nuisance animal control work, some for a fee, and may remove one, and sometimes more, problem animals. Nevertheless, when it comes to bounties paid on a number of coyotes, tax dollars are usually spent for nothing.

In an earlier chapter I discussed the bounties that some states and provinces enacted many years ago in an attempt to reduce coyotes. Heck, at one time there were bounties on numerous predators, including wolves, mountain lions, bears, and bobcats, as well as woodchucks (groundhogs) and many other rodents. Even crows had prices on their heads, and at one time, I can remember two cents being paid for every pigeon by a county not far from me in Indiana. In the 1960s numerous pigeons had become more than mere nuisances; their droppings had become a health hazard.

You can just imagine how some poor folks might have jumped at the chance to make a few bucks by going after Wily one on one. When officials first placed a price on the coyote, they assumed that the predators would be controlled at minimal cost. Wow! They were way off on that one.

Bounty hunting may have consequences that few of us anticipate. Charles Cadieux, in *Coyotes: Predators and Survivors*, discussed a summary provided by Don Balser, who had a long and distinguished career with the U.S. Fish and Wildlife Service after working for the Minnesota department. His summary first appeared in Minnesota Informational Leaflet No. 1 in 1958.

1. Too few predators are bountied to bring about reduction of the breeding stock, so that the whole population can be reduced.
2. The bounty system results in unnecessary payments— payments are being made for predators that would have been killed anyway, without the bounty.
3. The bounty system is a shotgun approach, aimed at an entire species across an entire state, and does not get at the animal causing the economic loss.
4. Bounty systems are invitations to fraud. House cats are bountied as bobcats, dogs as coyotes or wolves . . . and scalps are transported from low-pay to high-pay states.
5. The bounty system encourages "farming" of predators. Some trappers bounty the males and the pups, letting the female go free to produce more bounty-eligible animals for next year.

Those are just five of Balser's summary points, but his message is clear. If there's a buck to be made, somebody is going to try to pull a fast one to make it. For just a moment, imagine hunters raising more coyotes, just so they can be paid more bounties. And what about an individual who would take his bounty across a state line to get paid a higher rate? You see, at one time South Dakota paid twice as much as North Dakota did for coyotes. We can also speculate on the number of animals that are "salvaged." In other words, what's to stop a guy from picking up a road-killed coyote, scalping it, and turning it in for bounty money?

Two more questions about the bounty system come to my mind. First, who is to say that the dead coyote for which someone just got paid, with your tax dollars, is the one that caused the problem? And second, is paying bounties on coyotes an economical solution to a problem? To give you an example, Michigan dished out $1.8 million between 1935 and 1970 for 111,569 coyotes. There's still a bunch of coyotes in Michigan, and they still do damage.

Paying bounties for animals began in Massachusetts in the 1600s, but no bounties were offered for coyotes. Coyote bounties began with the territorial expansion across the Mississippi River. Have bounties done any good? Let's see. I won't provide figures in dollars, because that may not provide a fair answer. In other words, $25,000 might have been paid for coyotes in 1930, and $50,000 in 1940; however, the state that paid the bounties may have upped the value of coyotes during the 10-year period. Maybe they once paid $3 per predator, but then raised it to $5. For this reason, I'll talk numbers of coyotes killed. For example, in 1898 more than 5,500 coyotes were bountied in North Dakota. In the late 1940s hunters bountied more than 11,000 coyotes. Now stop and think about that. If bounty hunting suc-

TEXAS WOLF AND BOUNTY ACT

(1892)

That the county commissioners of the several counties within the State may issue county warrants to the person killing in any amount not exceeding $3 for every wolf, coyote, wildcat, and fox; and 5 cents for each rabbit that shall be captured and killed in the said county. No person shall be entitled to receive any bounty as set forth in section one without first making it appear by positive proof by affidavit in writing, filed with the county clerk, that the wolf, coyote, wildcat, rabbit, or fox was captured or killed within the limits of the county in which the application was made. This act shall not apply

to counties having a total property valuation of less than $500,000, and shall not be in force until ordered by the board of county commissioners.

Reprinted from *The Clever Coyote* by Stanley P. Young and Hartley H. T. Jackson.

cessfully reduces the number of coyotes, shouldn't it have done so in 40 years? Instead, there were twice as many coyotes bountied in the 1940s as there was when bounty hunting was initiated in the state. Of course, the higher figure may only reflect an increase in the number of successful bounty hunters in the state, rather than an increase in the number of coyotes. Still, either way, it's clear that the bounty system did not reduce North Dakota's coyote population.

One Michigan report did indicate that coyote numbers might have dropped for a while during its bounty program. In 1936, 2,904 bounties were paid out for coyotes. In 1939, the number dropped to 2,066, and by 1942 only 1,501 bounties were paid. By 1944, though, the bounty numbers reached an all-time high at 2,869. In 1945 the state paid for 3,278 coyotes, and that was only through November.

Today few, if any, states or provinces pay bounties for coyotes. There may be a couple of stragglers still doing so, but for the most part these money-wasting programs have been halted. Have we finally gotten the message?

Furthermore, bounties cannot ensure that the targeted animal is actually the one that's killed. It should be understood that not all coyotes become killers of pets and livestock. When it comes to the coyote's easy targets, such as sheep or household pets, various factors influence coyote depredation. Wildlife biologists Knowlton and Gese said that behavioral differences among coyotes might influence their likelihood to kill. This suggests that not all coyotes kill sheep, and those individuals that do will kill sometimes but not others. Several California studies report numerous radio-collared coyotes in the vicinity of sheep with few, if any, recorded losses of lambs. In these studies, most confirmed coyote kills were directly attributable to predation by breeding, territorial coyotes, while other coyotes appeared to be innocuous. In another study 6 of 11 coyotes removed by aerial gunning on four ranches in Montana showed evidence of having depredated sheep. Similarly, in an unexploited coyote population, biologists determined that 65 percent of the coyotes exposed to a herd of goats fed upon them even though the goats were present for only 21 days. It isn't known how many of these coyotes were involved in actually killing the goats, but more than 40 percent of the kids in the herd were killed.

My point is, when and if you decide to become the vigilante, it's easier than you think to place the end of the rope around the wrong neck. Granted, that's not so bad in the eyes of some. Many folks don't really care if "that" coyote committed the crime; there are no "innocent" coyotes, so they believe. Other folks, though, demand justice only when they know beyond any doubt that the guilty party was caught.

In the early 1900s the "government trapper" was born. There were several thousand trappers, all employed by the federal government to find and trap predators—most often coyotes. However, make no mistake: These individuals knew their stuff. Poorly paid? Probably. A qualified trapper and outdoorsman? Absolutely. Government trappers knew everything about coyotes, and spent many days in the bush living with them. They also had appreciation and great respect for this predator.

Many times, a government trapper was sent after one lamb-killing coyote only. Some government trappers even pursued coyote dens.

Yes, den hunting may be another lethal option, providing that it's legal in the area where you'll search for a coyote den.

Before proceeding, check your local regulations or talk with an official. It may sound inhuman, but many have claimed it has put a stop to problem coyotes killing livestock and even pets. The primary reason for den hunting is to eradicate the pups. Once the pups are gone, the male and female no longer have to feed them. Thus, livestock cease being killed and pets no longer disappear.

Is den hunting cruel? Yes, to some extent. Of course, that's my opinion. Others who have major problems with coyotes will probably disagree. More than likely, if you think it's cruel it's because you imagine the cute little pups being handed the death

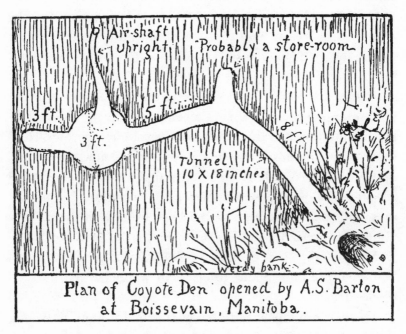

Plan of Coyote Den opened by A.S. Barton at Boissevain, Manitoba.

Mating coyotes often use the same den one breeding season after another.

sentence. I don't quite look at it that way—killing pups in the den may be more humane, in the long run, than killing their parents. If the mating pair of coyotes were killed instead, the pups would be left alone with no parents to protect and feed them. To some degree den hunting is an effective means of gaining temporary relief from problem coyotes, but as discussed previously, the more coyotes you take, the more coyotes are made.

ADC (Animal Damage Control) has used various methods to kill nuisance coyotes, from traps and snares to shooting from aircraft. In 1988 the government removed 75,869 coyotes. By 1991 the annual number surpassed 95,000. However, ADC had no qualms about eradicating problem coyotes. All of these coyotes were targeted animals that were responsible for a variety of damages. Some also had become a public safety threat. Many folks who suffered damages also had no qualms about the removal of the targeted coyotes. In thousands of instances where coyotes were killed, damages stopped totally or declined considerably.

If you do choose the lethal alternative, one option you probably won't consider is aerial gunning for coyotes. Most folks don't have a Cessna sitting around waiting to go coyote hunting. I also doubt you'll run out and buy an airplane just to use in the hunting of coyotes, although some folks have spent much more attempting to eradicate these predators.

I'm not sure who came up with the idea of aerial gunning, but it was first attempted in the early 1920s. Things got off to a shaky start for lone pilots who tried it (it wasn't easy flying and shooting simultaneously), but as time passed, practice made perfect. Eventually, most aerial coyote hunts were undertaken by a pilot and a shooter. One source noted that an aerial hunter killed 113 coyotes in 1931.

Pilots usually found it necessary to fly at a ceiling of 300 feet (sometimes lower), and they had to be good pilots to maneuver around and over hills and timber. Nonetheless, aerial coyote hunting was hazardous. Pilots and gunners were occasionally killed.

As aerial hunting became commonplace, many coyotes wised up and learned to dive into brush and hide whenever a plane came near. Some coyotes practiced their dodging skills merely upon hearing a plane coming.

Although aerial gunning has resulted in thousands of dead coyotes, it hasn't stopped problems from occurring. First, consider that not all targeted coyotes can be hunted down and killed. Aerial hunting isn't possible in a suburb of Philadelphia where a coyote just ran off with a kitty clamped in his jaws, nor is it possible in wild brushy habitats where coyotes often prey upon livestock. Nevertheless, at one time there was another lethal alternative to gunning. It was called Compound 1080.

Compound 1080 is actually sodium monofluoroacetate, a deadly poison. It was first used to eradicate coyotes in the 1940s. However, Compound 1080 is no longer an option for controlling coyotes. In 1972 President Richard Nixon signed an executive order banning Compound 1080 from federal lands and programs.

Compound 1080 is tasteless and odorless. When used to eradicate coyotes, it was placed in bait—often a dead sheep, or just a pile of meat. After ingesting the white powder, the animal's nervous system was severely affected, usually causing him to run "haywire."

You might think that Compound 1080 was outlawed on federal lands primarily because it was a poison that caused coyotes an agonizing death. Nope. The real reason is that many folks claimed that too many *other* species of animals would suffer the same agonizing death that was meant for Wily and associates.

Proponents of Compound 1080 claim only canines will feed upon the baits, pointing out that felines seldom eat carrion, and therefore wouldn't be affected by the poison. Furthermore, they insist, if people penned their dogs, they wouldn't have to fear their accidental deaths. In fact, no evidence exists that proves Compound 1080 has ever killed scavengers and predators other than coyotes. But we do know that Compound 1080 did reduce coyote numbers for a period of many years in the western U.S.

The average person should forgo any thoughts about using poison, though. Legality is an essential issue, and other risks make it too dangerous to consider. All poisons threaten the lives of other animals and birds, and they also pose serious threats to human health and safety.

If you choose to eradicate, there are two types of eradication to realistically think about. First, you can choose to get rid of one particular coyote. Second, you can attempt to reduce the overall number of coyotes in a particular area. The decision probably depends upon the extent of damage you've suffered. If you have an occasional problem, removing one individual may suffice. If you're losing several livestock animals to predation, then it may be beneficial to reduce the number of coyotes in the area.

If you target only one coyote, there will be less work involved. (Note: I did not say "little or no work" involved.) If you choose to make a dent in the coyote population, you should plan your strategy carefully. A livestock producer should remove coyotes in late winter and early spring, before lambing and calving begin.

You may rid yourself of a problem coyote or two by taking lethal measures, but be aware that the coyote has a way of quickly learning to avoid them and sharpening his survival techniques. When poisons were used, coyotes learned to avoid the bait. In many situations, they wised up and didn't eat what was offered. Start shooting at them and you may have success for a while; however, you'll be surprised how quickly your shooting opportunities vanish, even though coyotes are still residing in the area. Yes, the coyote has an uncanny way of figuring things out. Every eradication method you employ will only be temporarily effective. That you can count on. That's also why many folks look more closely at preventive and nonlethal options than they do eradication methods.

There's one last consideration before making up your mind whether or not to eradicate a coyote. Think back to the early days when settlers axed their way through this continent. They worried about the major beasts, such as bears, mountain lions, and wolves. Coyotes were there all along, but didn't worry them. Over time, most of the large predators were wiped out or pushed into isolated wilderness areas. Since then, governments and other folks have tried everything imaginable to do the same to coyotes, but these costly endeavors don't work. There are now more coyotes than ever, and it appears likely that the problems they cause will only increase, despite large numbers of the predator being killed over the years.

8

Coping with Urban Coyotes

QUESTION: How many pounds will a coyote weigh when he grows up?

ANSWER: I'd say about 150 pounds.
                    —Bradley Williams, age 6

Thank goodness, adult coyotes aren't quite as heavy as 150 pounds. Imagine the catastrophes they'd create satisfying their hunger pains. No longer would livestock, poultry, and pets be primarily at risk of attack. Instead, it would be joggers, hikers, other outdoorsmen, bicyclists, mail carriers, pedestrians, and all those folks standing at a bus stop. Of course, it would also be more difficult for coyotes to hide, and they couldn't be as sneaky as the 30- and 40-pound coyotes we commonly deal with.

Before getting into nonlethal and lethal control methods for coyotes that attack livestock, I think it best to pass along a little advice about preventive measures and urban coyotes. After all, if you could lead a coyote away from temptation, you wouldn't have to worry about him—although it's improbable that you ever could. Nevertheless, you might divert him from the kinds of thoughts that get him into trouble.

Controlling coyotes in urban areas differs considerably from controlling those in rural areas. In most cases, the hunting and trapping of coyotes is prohibited within the limits of metropolitan districts. Most folks must therefore resort to preventing coyote damage before it occurs or resort to scare tactics, such as noisemakers, throwing rocks, or a few other tricks I'll pass along in the pages that follow.

There's no single preventive measure that works on all coyotes, urban and rural. First, consider that personalities of individual coyotes differ considerably. In addition, since they inflict many kinds of damages, you can't assume that one method of control will work to stop every coyote. You must consider a variety of preventive measures, and pick out the most likely strategy. If the strategy you employ doesn't work, consider one of the other control options from a later chapter. If you get desperate and want to do away with Wily, read the chapter that discusses lethal control methods. If you just want to send the coyote back to the western plains where he can sing "Home on the Range," then read the shipping instructions for United Parcel Service and the postal service.

In all honesty, outwitting an urban coyote begins with damage prevention. It shouldn't begin with a plan to kill the predator, nor with a plan to control and outsmart him. You see, once a coyote causes damage the first time, it gets easier for him to do it again. When it comes to killing, you could compare him to a serial killer. With each successive kill, it gets harder and harder for you to stop him.

The following methods are recommended primarily for folks in suburban and metropolitan areas who have less severe problems than rural and wilderness dwellers who experience major livestock losses. I do realize that a pet may be more valuable to you than Farmer Hansen's 22 lambs, 14 goats, and 9 calves that cost him a few months' salary, so I'll take no shortcuts when providing ideas. I'll give you all the preventive information that's known to science—and some that isn't.

Protecting Pets

If Fido disappeared last week, this chapter came too late for you. But if you just took Fido out, and spotted a coyote near the back alley where Fido hangs out occasionally, you may be reading this chapter in the nick of time.

Coyotes commonly invade urban areas and steal pets. For instance, a Las Vegas newspaper reported the rising frequency of coyote encounters in the city. The expansion of homes into what was once their rangeland has forced coyotes to do some of their hunting in the subdivisions. And Las Vegas is not unusual. Coyotes have invaded the suburbs of many cities. A news report from the Colorado Division of Wildlife warned Denver pet owners that area cats and dogs were under great risk of attack from coyotes. Cats had become prey; dogs were usually attacked because coyotes considered them territorial intruders.

When it comes to preying on pets, coyotes probably take more cats than dogs, although small dogs are often killed. (In some rare instances coyotes kill large dogs.) Owners, unfortunately, may never know that a coyote took their cat or dog since coyotes usually carry small pets away. They also have an efficient way of surgically skinning the animal, which leaves little of their prey left for identification. Coyotes kill other types of pets, too, including rabbits.

Most coyotes that begin killing pets usually did not, at first, consider them prey. Often, they were attracted to areas where pets hang out. Eventually, this attraction—usually food—may lead them to kill a pet. If you think that Wily doesn't like kitty and dog food, dry or right out of the can, you're in for a big surprise.

One way you might deduce that a coyote has moved into the area and is eating your pet's food is if you notice more food missing than usual. More than likely, if your pet's food bowl used to have some left each time you fed him, and now it's always gone, you can bet that something else is eating it. Many wild critters, including the coyote, would gladly eat a bowl of pet food. Of course, most of the free-roaming dogs and cats in the area are eager to share Fido's dinner, too. However, if water is available along with the pet food, you just might be making Wily one sated coyote every night.

To avoid feeding coyotes involuntarily, feed and water your pet indoors. If that isn't possible, regulate your pet's food so that there's no waste. The smell of any leftovers may attract a coyote. For this reason, bring in an empty food bowl each night. Further, always store your pet food indoors. It wouldn't make much sense to empty the pet's dish, and then leave a 25-pound bag of kibble sitting on the back porch.

You also want to avoid feeding stray animals. If you have an occasional kitty coming up to the porch after dark every evening, it's very tempting to give the rascal a few scraps or a little cat food. Of course, you already know the risk. The pet food, or the pet, may attract a coyote.

If you allow your pet to roam, he could become coyote bait at any time. In many areas, leash laws exist that outlaw free-roaming pets; however, even if your pet is restricted to a fenced backyard, he's hardly safe from a coyote. Your best bet is to keep your pets indoors, particularly at night. If the pet stays outside in a fenced yard or a kennel, make certain there are no openings under the fence. Coyotes are adept at wriggling under fences (or digging under them), and can squeeze under the slightest opening. Simply chaining or leashing your dog to keep him from wandering while outdoors will not protect him from coyotes. They will come to your dog. Pet remains have been found still attached to chains and leashes.

The best protection you can provide for your pet is a pen. A chain-link fence (livestock fencing is seldom feasible because of its large openings), or other type of fence with tightly woven wire, such as a welded-wire or woven-wire fencing at least 5 to 6 feet tall, should overlap a floor of wood or concrete. If a floor isn't possible, then you should bury the fence under the ground at least 18 inches since, as mentioned previously, coyotes will dig under fences to get to your pet. Even if the ground is so hard that you have to work an hour or two to dig a fence-post hole a couple of feet down, assume that a coyote can dig it out in a few minutes. Coyotes are also excellent jumpers, and can easily leap over a 4-foot fence. They occasionally climb fences, but not as readily as do foxes.

For your pet's protection—and your own, for that matter—never allow a coyote to come close to your pet. If one approaches your pet, do your best to intimidate him with noise. If you do nothing at all and the coyote is somewhat used to people, he may very well continue to approach. If you see coyotes frequently in the area, and you often put your pet on a leash and take him for a walk, do so only in daylight hours. You should also vaccinate your pets regularly for rabies, distemper, and other diseases that sometimes affect dogs and cats.

Yard Modifications

If you have any brush piles or woodpiles in the yard, I suggest you dispose of them. This debris attracts rodents, which will attract coyotes. The same goes for dense cover surrounding the yard. If thickets border your yard, it's an invitation to many nocturnal animals, which the coyote preys upon. Naturally, it would be best if you keep your grass cut. If you allow your grass to grow tall, perhaps 6 inches or more, it will attract mice and meadow voles. Wily will love you for this, because mice and voles taste almost as good as kitty cats and puppy dogs.

You'll also want to trim the lower limbs of trees in your yard, and keep your shrubs trimmed. Thick conifer trees provide coyotes with excellent habitat and a place to hide.

A coyote that stays primarily nocturnal and is somewhat used to people will often spend his days laid up in opportune locations near your home. For this reason, crawl spaces under outbuildings, porches, and decks should be closed off. In addition, a nearby drainpipe that stays dry most of the time will provide an excellent place for a coyote to lay up. If a culvert is close to your home and you've had coyote problems, or fear you soon will have, talk to local officials to see what they can do to make certain a coyote won't be able to use the drainpipe as a den or refuge.

To reduce the chance of a coyote showing up in the yard, turn on lights at night. You can also make noises, providing you get along with the neighbors. If coyotes frequently get into the yard, I recommend building a fence. As suggested earlier, use a net-wire type and avoid field fencing, which may have openings of 6 inches. Coyotes can squeeze through the tightest of openings. An ideal height is about 5 to 6 feet, but you may want to install an arch on top of the fence (made from other fencing) that leans away from the yard. The outward arch should include three strands of wire and extend at least 12 inches. This will deter coyotes from climbing over it. And again, you should bury the fence 18 inches to prevent a coyote from digging and coming under it.

If you decide to install a fence around the yard, you might want to convince your neighbors to do the same. The more fences, the merrier and safer you and your pets will be.

Bird Feeders, Garbage, and Compost

It only makes sense that bird feed, garbage, and compost will draw coyotes. Pet food attracts coyotes, so why wouldn't other types of foods (especially those with strong odors)? As for bird feed, though, it isn't necessarily the seeds that coyotes are looking to feast upon. Birdseed tempts a wide variety of critters into our yards, and they lure Wily in after them.

To provide some measure of protection against Wily, put up only feeders designed specifically for birds. Keep them well above the ground and clean up any excess seed that drops around them. Seed buildup attracts rodents and, therefore, coyotes. If the occasion offers, Wily can feast on a full backyard meal. A nice fat mouse serves as appetizer, and Fluffy the cat (who was lured there by the mouse) becomes the main course.

Birds also follow the seed to the ground, but although Wily might pounce on one occasionally as a tasty dessert, coyotes eat far fewer birds than they do mice and other rodents.

Keep in mind, however, that free-roaming cats are attracted to both the birds and the rodents. After killing a sparrow or a vole, a cat will often drag it a short distance away, and then leave the remains behind for a scavenger. The partially scavenged animal provides Wily with a well-balanced meal. Therefore, if coyotes have been sighted in your neighborhood, it's probably safest to remove the bird feeder. If the sightings stop, you can return the bird feeder outdoors.

Even more widely available to coyotes is garbage. What more can I say? Wily dearly loves to jump headfirst in a garbage can, or rip into a four-ply trash bag stuffed with goodies. After all, garbage is free, it's easy, and it's there for the taking. Wily only needs to wait until the middle of the night when all is quiet to get the garbage.

If you don't find coyote tracks or scat, there's no definitive way to tell if it *was* a coyote that got into your garbage can, though. Usually, garbage strewn over a distance tells you that "something" got into the can. Neighborhood pets routinely rummage through refuse; however, if you find garbage dragged into a dense area nearby, it could be the work of Wily or another wild animal. Most free-roaming pets sort through the garbage on location.

Securing garbage bags and containers and preventing coyotes from eating your trash is pretty straightforward. Obviously, you shouldn't leave bags of trash sitting by the door or piled up out in the yard. If you can keep all garbage in a building or garage that has no door open for a coyote, then you won't have any problems. If you must keep garbage outside, it should be placed in a large, heavy-duty container, preferably a metal one. You should also secure the lid with an elastic strap (a bicycle strap or a bungee cord works well), stretching it over the top and attaching it from handle to handle. If possible, don't place your garbage in its pickup location the night before it's picked up. Instead, do it early in the morning. The coyote will have less time to do his scavenging, and he'll be forced to do it in daylight hours.

Since coyotes are strong and will often get up on their back legs to reach higher, your garbage can should be secured to the ground, or to the side of a building. Yet even if you secure the lid, a coyote might pick up odors and turn a can over, doing everything he can to get inside. You might invest in a trash-can holder on wheels. These nifty devices keep the can from tipping, and they make it easy to move your garbage to pickup areas.

Depending upon its contents, compost often attracts coyotes. Compost consisting of only foliage and rotting leaves has no appeal to a coyote, but if the compost consists of manure, animal meat or parts, or fresh or rotting fruit and vegetables, its scent will draw coyotes to it. So be careful never to compost anything that will attract coyotes, and always cover compost piles with heavy tarps.

If you have fruit trees growing in your yard, keep the ground under them clean. Rotting apples, peaches, plums, pears, and other fruits will attract coyotes and rodents. Coyotes would be happy to gorge on either mice or plums.

About 45,000 words ago, I mentioned that you might never know that a coyote was living under your doorstep. If you have read this book in its entirety, you'll consider that statement a fact.

Human Health and Safety

Rabies in coyotes is rare. Nevertheless, in south Texas a state health emergency was declared in 1994, and by 1995 a statewide rabies quarantine had been put into effect. The epidemic got its start in 1988, when two counties confirmed canine rabies in 11 domestic dogs and 6 coyotes. Three years later cases were reported in 10 more counties as far north as 100 miles away from the first ones. Another 10 counties reported rabid animals during the next 3½ years. More than 600 rabies cases were documented in a 20-county area from 1988 to 1995.

Laboratory-Confirmed Rabies Cases in 20 South Texas Counties from 1988 to 1995

Species	Total Confirmed Rabies Cases
Coyotes	327
Dogs	245
Raccoons	25
Cats	21
Cows	15
Bobcats	5
Horses	4
Goats	1
Skunks	1
Total	**644**

As well as rabies, coyotes carry other diseases that may be transmitted to pets, although they seldom pose threats to humans. Distemper, parvovirus, and mange are the most common. Mange is a contagious skin condition caused by small parasites called mites, which are similar to the chiggers that bury in the skin of humans. Animals usually contract mange in early spring when their fur is thin. Coyotes, and any other wild animals with mange for that matter, should be destroyed before they have a chance to pass the disease to pets.

Most dog owners are familiar with distemper. Coyotes have been diagnosed with distemper, but these incidents are infrequent. The disease begins as a virus and is transmitted from one animal to another by direct contact. Once infected with distemper, an animal displays odd behavior, similar to rabies symptoms, and may express fearlessness toward humans. It may have a discharge of saliva and secretions around the eyes. Any coyote with distemper should be destroyed to prevent spread of the disease.

Coyotes, regardless of where they are, may also carry ticks and Lyme disease. Most folks in metropolitan areas shouldn't be unduly alarmed, although people living in rural areas have a significant risk of contracting the disease, especially if they don't take precautions.

Lyme disease, named for the Connecticut town where it was first detected, is an infection caused by *Borrelia burgdorferi*, a member of the family of spirochetes, or corkscrew-shaped bacteria. A tick known as the deer tick carries this bacterium. Its official name is *Ixodes dammini,* commonly found in the north-central and northeastern states. Another close cousin is *I. pacificus*, which resides in many western states. The deer tick feeds on many mammals and birds, but white-tailed deer and rodents seem to be favorites. Of course, you should understand that these animal hosts do not directly pass the disease to humans. The tick spreads the disease, and if an infected one falls from an animal host and attaches to a human, the individual could contract Lyme disease.

It's believed that an infected tick must remain attached to a human for at least 48 hours before the disease can be contracted. An array of symptoms may follow, including a bull's-eye rash around the bite, and some pain and redness. Flu-like symptoms sometimes follow, and in severe cases (several weeks or months later) arthritislike pain in one or more joints.

Coyotes carry numerous ticks, as do dogs and other pets; however, we don't know if coyotes are at risk for Lyme disease, although dogs have been diagnosed with it. The most frequent carriers of Lyme disease could be mice. Since coyotes are attracted to rodents such as mice, they are therefore often lured into tick-infested areas where they may come in contact with tick-infested prey. And coyotes often venture from rural areas into metropolitan areas, bringing ticks with them. Once the tick stuffs its gut with the coyote's blood, it drops to the ground. That could be anywhere—the coyote's den on the edge of town, a few miles into the countryside, or in your backyard while you're snoozing in the middle of the night.

Some ticks also carry bacteria that cause Rocky Mountain spotted fever in humans. The organism, *Rickettsia rickettsii*, is transmitted by the common wood tick or dog tick. Coyotes also carry their share of wood ticks into metropolitan areas. Today Rocky Mountain spotted fever has been confirmed in almost every state in the United States.

Rocky Mountain spotted fever may take longer to show up than Lyme disease, sometimes not until months after contracting the disease. In most cases, though, symptoms will show up within a few days of being bitten by the tick carrying the disease. Early symptoms include headaches and fever, and many times a red rash appears and then spreads over the body. Fortunately, although the disease is aggressive, it's seldom fatal in humans. Only about 2 percent of those who contract the fever will die. Rocky Mountain spotted fever and Lyme disease are usually treated with antibiotics.

For your own protection, you should remove weeds and brush surrounding your yard. This will reduce the number of mice, coyotes, and other animals that could host disease-carrying ticks. Chemicals can also be used around the home, garden, and lawn to kill ticks, but make certain you contact a pest control professional because they're toxic.*

Fear of Coyotes and Preventing Attack

Although the right coyote could attack any human on the wrong day, chances are it never will. Coyotes are not out to get you. Even if you try to provoke a coyote into attacking, you'll probably fail no matter how aggressive the coyote, or how determined you are to force an attack. Although officials have documented several cases, coyote attacks on humans are rare. Children, because of their size, are at the greatest risk. Coyotes have dragged

---

*For more information on ticks and Lyme disease, see *Outwitting Ticks* by Susan Carol Hauser (The Lyons Press, 2001).

children out of backyards, and have attacked them even when adults were present.

Although many coyote attacks on humans have been serious and led to extensive medical care, most attack victims are treated and released with minor injuries. Only one coyote fatality has been documented: a three-year-old California girl. Nevertheless, even an attack that results in only minor injuries could require rabies vaccinations.

Since children are at a much greater risk of attack than adults, it's important that brushy habitat not be available around children's play areas, such as backyards, parks, or school playgrounds. Any vegetation—wild or ornamental—should be reduced to a minimum in areas bordering play areas. When dense cover is removed, a coyote cannot sneak in and make a surprise attack. Removing brush will also reduce the number of rodents surrounding the area, and with fewer rodents present, coyotes are less likely to nose around. Coyotes also visit golf courses, but since children seldom do, there's little concern of a coyote attack occurring in them.

Although limiting vegetation reduces risks of coyote attacks, many folks would rather leave the habitat. No doubt, providing a hospitable environment for critters will increase wildlife viewing opportunities. Therefore, if it means more to you to observe wildlife than to protect yourself and others, by all means leave the habitat alone. I would much rather build habitat than destroy it, even though I have lost numerous livestock animals to coyotes and other species of predators. The benefits of having animals nearby outweigh the losses. On the other hand, if an animal threatens your family, do not hesitate to do away with the habitat it calls home.

Naturally, it's not a good idea to leave children unattended. Always make sure someone is watching them, and keep them confined to a limited play area. A small child often looks like prey to a coyote, and an adult in a crouched position may look like prey. For this reason, if you're out working in the yard and are bent over, make sure you stand up if you see a coyote nearby.

When you observe a coyote, pay close attention to its behavior. Does it appear healthy? Does it walk normally? Does it seem to have a fear of people? If you answer "no" to any of these questions, report the animal to authorities immediately. That could be an animal damage control agency, a law enforcement division, or a conservation officer.

When a coyote expresses little fear of people, try to scare it away. Noises may work, but make certain you don't end up in jail trying to run off a coyote—your county may have a noise ordinance. Honk your car's horn, bang pots and pans together, set off a portable air horn or siren, or holler loudly. Many coyotes will run immediately upon hearing loud noises, but unfortunately, some might not. If you run into a stubborn coyote, don't necessarily assume that he's about to attack. Use common sense and don't approach the coyote; he may just be used to people and noises.

Throw rocks at a coyote that refuses to leave, or fire a slingshot at him. If the law permits, you can shoot him with a pellet gun. You must believe that "sticks and stones can break his bones, but slingshots and pellet guns might hurt even more." Yet if the noise and projectiles still haven't scared him off, consider running at a coyote. Even the most stubborn coyote that expresses no fear of people will come unglued when you run directly at him, yelling as you approach. If the coyote doesn't run, stop, get clear of the animal, and call the authorities.

If a coyote ends up in your yard and appears reluctant to move, grab the garden hose and spray him with water. More than likely, he'll take off like he just spotted a roadrunner.

If you'd like to set up a scarecrow to frighten a coyote, go right ahead; however, be aware that it will do absolutely no good. Scarecrows scare crows, but they don't frighten coyotes. The only exception would be a moving scarecrow. You can pick up a slightly used 4-foot robot for about $120,000. Keep it patrolling your yard all night and you can count on keeping the coyotes at bay.

Do you need to coyote-proof your house? Absolutely not. If your house has closed doors and windows, it's a coyote-proof house.

We've all heard of or seen signs such as DON'T FEED THE BEARS. Today new signs have been posted in some areas that warn DON'T FEED THE COYOTES. Yet in some national parks visitors still throw food to coyotes. Some even tempt coyotes to take food out of their hands.

We know for a fact that some coyotes attacked people only after they were once fed by humans. In many cases, humans had fed coyotes just before the attack occurred. Nobody could say for sure that feeding the coyote was a direct cause of the attack; however, we do know that feeding a coyote will tame the animal somewhat. We also know that it will make a coyote dependent upon humans. Once a coyote stops hunting on his own and loses his fear of people, he becomes dangerous and could attack without warning.

In Vancouver, British Columbia—a heavily populated metropolitan district where approximately 2,000 coyotes also reside—a coyote was shot and killed after biting a young girl and killing

Feeding coyotes may just make them so comfortable with people that they put both themselves and humans in danger.

several pets. An autopsy revealed that the animal had dined on a meal of cooked chicken shortly before it was killed.

Assume that a fed coyote is a dead coyote. Once a predator loses his fear of people, he'll probably end up in serious trouble. Officials won't give a coyote a second chance if he becomes a threat to humans. Instead, the animal will be promptly destroyed.

Coyotes don't need help from humans to survive. Even in urban locations, where they may not prey upon as many wild animals as they do in rural areas, they will manage to get by without your help. And don't think for a moment that feeding a coyote will reduce the chance of him wanting to eat a kitty or two. Feeding a coyote will only put you and your pet at greater risk.

Most people are afraid of coyotes. Just spotting one in areas inhabited by humans will raise eyebrows, send hearts pounding, and spark up a lot of conversations. Because of this, many counties and towns have made it a point to educate the public about coyotes. If an incident occurs, such as a coyote attacking a pet or, worse a human, most town officials will immediately take action. In the winter of 1997 a coyote was suspected of killing a poodle in Oak Creek, Wisconsin. After hearing complaints from area dog owners, Milwaukee County officials proposed shooting any problem coyotes. Department of Natural Resource wildlife managers and a conservation officer then met with the community leaders to discuss coyote biology and management. After the discussions, the shooting program was abandoned due to public opposition.

Permits to trap nuisance coyotes were issued in Racine County in 1995 and 1996; however, the trapping program was stalled until 1997 after a legal trap caught a pet owner's dog. Eventually, the state did allow coyote trapping without the need for a permit.

There's a compelling reason for coyotes to venture into urban areas: They've learned that they're safe from hunting and trapping. Humans are natural predators, feared by all wild animals, including ferocious beasts that could easily kill an adult. Nevertheless, if a coyote isn't pursued as a game animal by nature's number one predators, his natural fear of humans will decrease.

A Need for Education

Often, urban dwellers know little about coyotes. Nonetheless, they move into the countryside, and often attempt to become, as one biologist put it, "wildlife stewards." Some of them even attempt to become wildlife stewards in metropolitan districts, after they begin consistently seeing wildlife. Today that's nothing new, thanks to humankind's expansion deeper into animal habitats. Most people, however, simply aren't qualified wildlife experts, and they have little understanding or knowledge of coyotes. Many turn to city and county officials, but soon discover that some of these folks don't have answers either. Yet, as we continue seeing more coyotes and other wild animals entering the suburbs and urban areas, a need has arisen to educate both the public and public officials. Therefore, studies have been undertaken to determine the best way to do this.

Kristine Lampa's thesis directly addresses this need. She named the coyote an ideal "flagship" species for urban wildlife education programs. According to Lampa, the coyote even has a "captivating urban personality" that offers an educational opportunity and a challenge for us. Can we live with the untamed creatures that share our cities? The following are eight recommendations that Lampa provided to Vancouver. These recommendations could also apply to other metropolitan areas:

1. Incorporate public opinion when formulating management approaches for coyotes and other urban wildlife. Also, use it as a means of assessing the progress and acceptance of such programs.

2. Use public education and other nonlethal methods for addressing urban wildlife problems. Public education is an important tool for the management of urban coyotes because traditional wildlife management techniques are not feasible or publicly acceptable in cities.

3. Target educational materials to particular segments of the population, such as parents with young children and pet owners. It may be practical to target pet owners at veterinary clinics.

4. Expand current "do not feed the wildlife" initiatives; this should help reduce conflicts between coyotes and people.

5. Enforce municipal bylaws that discourage the public from feeding wildlife.

6. Different agencies that deal with urban wildlife should collaborate promoting a coordinated approach and consistent message in addressing coyotes and other urban wildlife. This would reduce duplication and make information more accessible and consistent for the public.

7. Clarification of the roles of different agencies that directly and indirectly deal with coyotes and other urban wildlife would be useful for the public.

8. Agencies should become more actively involved in working with the media to distribute valid information

about coyotes, because the vast majority of people get their information about wildlife from television.

According to Lampa's survey, 613 coyotes were sighted in Vancouver. Although they were spotted during both the day and at night, most were seen in the daytime. Individual coyotes were sighted a majority of the time (77 percent), but pairs and groups containing as many as nine coyotes were also reported. The greatest number of coyotes were spotted during the breeding season, between January and April, and the fewest during the dispersal season (September to December). Fifty percent of all urban coyote sightings occurred in parks, golf courses, and other open green spaces, and a mere 3 percent occurred in backyards and schoolyards.

Lampa also noted that urban coyotes appeared bolder when people were walking their dogs, although, in each case where a dog was in danger of attack, the coyote retreated when threatened by the pet's owner. Lampa also reported attacks on two young children in the Vancouver area. (See chapter 5.)

Urban wildlife education should begin with children. We should teach children to respect coyotes, and teach them that coyotes are wild animals that shouldn't be bothered. Children should learn that intervention, such as feeding coyotes or doing anything else to attract them, may result in the death of the coyote, or injury to humans.

Protecting Fruit and Vegetables

When garden vegetables consistently disappear a little each day, odds are you don't have a coyote problem. Raccoons and squirrels eat corn, and woodchucks (groundhogs) eat bean plants and other vegetables. Deer and rabbits eat a variety of garden plants. These animals get into a pattern of taking some each day, gradually widening their feeding zone in the garden. When a coyote attacks a garden, however, he's quick and decisive. He tears up most plants and eats the rest. Nevertheless, coyotes seldom damage gardens, unless fruits are grown in them. Coyotes dearly love melons, and they also eat pumpkins, grapes, blueberries, and strawberries, not to mention the fruits of trees, such as avocados, apples, pears, peaches, and plums.

If the rows between the vegetable plants are clean, you may find tracks that identify the animal doing the damage. To increase your chances of finding tracks, lay a couple of inches of sand or flour in targeted locations around the garden where the damage usually occurs. Five pounds of flour will cover three to four square feet and will pick up clear tracks, unless there's heavy overnight dew. Moisture can solidify flour or sand, wiping out a track that was once there.

A motion-activated light may help protect your garden area, but this is usually a temporary fix. As he will with noise, a coyote will get used to the light coming on each time he walks near. He may run away the first night and walk away the second, but if there's no additional deterrent, by the third or fourth night he'll be back in the garden with the light shining brightly.

Since coyotes are attracted to rotting vegetables and fruits, you should clean up your garden regularly. Any extremely ripe vegetables and fruits you don't intend to harvest should be disposed of instead of left on the ground. Growing fruits and vegetables you wish to protect from coyotes should be covered at night with a heavy tarp.

Consider erecting a coyote-proof fence around the garden. Although there are no fences labeled "coyote-proof" on the market, any fence that's (preferably) 6 feet tall, made of tightly woven or welded wire and is buried about 8 inches under the ground all the way around the garden, will keep out coyotes. You want fencing with small openings, usually 4 inches or smaller. Posts must be secured, and ideally set in concrete, or the fencing will give and slacken between posts. Some folks will go the extra mile by making an overhang above the fence that leans away from the area being protected. An overhang will keep a coyote from climbing the fence, or jumping over it. It can be made of barbed wire or a charged high-tensile wire. Nobody said it was easy, or inexpensive to set up a coyote-proof fence; however, they do work.

Short electric fences don't always work well against coyotes, but when you set them up properly with several strands, they can be effective. Many producers have used hot fences as physical barriers, and claim to have good results.

Coyotes will do whatever is necessary to get to something they want to eat—jump a fence or dig under it. They're always determined, and they don't like giving up. Nevertheless, there's another type of fencing for you to consider. It doesn't cost as much as conventional fences, and it doesn't require as much labor to set up. It's called the "electric peanut butter fence."

Peanut butter fences are often constructed to keep deer from getting to fruits, vegetables, shrubs, and trees; however, you could try the same construction pattern to ward off coyotes. A peanut butter fence is nothing more than an electric fence with short strips of aluminum foil wrapped around it, spaced every few feet. To make one, you'll need a few strands of wire spaced only about 6 inches apart and several strips of foil, each about 4 inches long. Attach them to the wires that extend around the area you want to protect, and daub each foil strip with peanut butter (make sure you do this *before* turning on the voltage).

Deer can't resist one lick of peanut butter, but the electric jolt deters lick number two. When they lick the foil and peanut butter the first time, they jump back a few feet and usually wander off to find less high-voltage treats. Will the peanut butter fence fool a coyote? Other animals have been attracted to peanut butter fences, and promptly discouraged, so why wouldn't a coyote be? He's more of an opportunist than most animals, including deer. Another reason for considering the peanut butter fence is that the coyote learns quickly. He won't forget that jolt, and he won't want to fool with the same fence again. That's good news for you.

To construct a simple electric fence, with the option of turning it into a peanut butter fence, place the bottom wire near the ground. Wily might choose to slip under a fence even if you have it only a few inches above the ground, but if you keep the fence low, odds are he'll scrape against it and get a shock. He may also be tempted to sample the peanut butter before going under the fence. In some cases, it may be necessary to construct a barbed wire above and below the hot wire. For more information on electric fences, see the following chapters about protecting livestock.

Another form of protection is human hair—its scent may ward off coyotes. You should spread the hair thickly around your garden or fruits, where the coyote can't miss coming into contact with it. To obtain an ample supply of human hair, visit a hair salon. Most hairdressers and barbers will gladly give away a hefty bag or two of hair. You can even offer to sweep it up for them.

Unfortunately, human hair is often only a temporary deterrent—if it works at all. Its human odor dissipates, especially after a rainfall, and the hair becomes nothing more than an eyesore on the ground. Further, many urban coyotes have no fear of human scent and will cross over the hair without giving it a second thought. Nonetheless, even animals accustomed to human scent usually don't like having it right under their noses. Thus, hair may still frighten away a coyote that consistently smells the scent of humans. Eventually, though, Wily will probably take the risk and trot right over the hair to get at food. It doesn't bite or grab him, so why not proceed with caution?

Other strong scents deter coyotes, too. Deodorant soaps placed around the perimeters of the garden may work. Soap may also discourage other wild animals that feast on your worldly grown goods.

No doubt, the urban coyote has caused a big fuss in recent years. Because of repeated problems, many citizens have demanded action from elected officials, and have been responsible for many emergency town meetings. Unfortunately, most officials have no safe, simple solution to the growing problem of urban coyotes. Shooting or trapping, though sometimes effective means of coyote control, usually aren't options in metropolitan areas. Tranquilizer darts also aren't an option, because of human safety and relocation problems. Why should your problem coyote be moved somewhere else and become someone else's pest? In addition, let's not forget that coyotes are territorial. If you do move a problem individual several miles out of the city, another will eventually take his place.

Although you may delay coyotes from coming into urban areas, this won't prevent their eventual invasion. No matter how hard you try, you can't stop a coyote from visiting and residing in an urban community. Coyotes learn fast, and they lose fears almost as quickly. The better educated you are about the predator, and the more you understand his needs and habits, the more tolerant of coyotes you'll be. As the coyote adjusts to suburbia, you must adjust to him, too. Simply said, you just find a way to live with your wild neighbor.

9

Protecting Livestock with Guard Animals

QUESTION: *What's the biggest problem we have with coyotes today?*

ANSWER: *They are very dangerous.*
                    —Brittaney Webster, age 14

Most livestock producers would tell you that coyotes have cost them a bundle of money. Nevertheless, relief for them is sometimes one phone call and one day away—that is, if they don't mind purchasing a guard animal. This investment might seem like pocket change if they've lost several head of livestock, several thousand smackers, and several nights of sleep.

Using guard animals to protect livestock is nothing new; it's been done for centuries. All you need is an animal that's more aggressive than the coyote. Guard animals have reduced livestock losses due to coyote predation, and they're more effective than scare devices. The most popular guard animals are llamas, dogs, and donkeys. Guard animals are used to protect all types of livestock, but are probably most popular with sheep producers.

Make no mistake: A pack of coyotes might defeat an attentive and aggressive guard animal. These incidents are rare but have occurred. Nevertheless, if you think that more is better and team up several guarding animals, it usually doesn't work. Guard animals generally don't get along with their own species, much less a different one. Forget about placing more than one guard animal with your livestock—unless you don't mind your pasture looking like a battlefield.

Guard Llamas

For many reasons, llamas are often more practical for protecting livestock than other animals. An Iowa State University study indicated that these animals are effective protectors of cattle, goats, and sheep. They have a natural desire to get aggressive with coyotes, and they're also hostile to dogs.

Researchers have pointed out several positive traits of llamas:

- They can be kept in fenced pastures.
- They don't require special feeding programs.
- They're very manageable.
- They have a long working life.
- They can see farther because they stand taller than other guard animals.
- They will bond with livestock in a matter of days.

Yet much more research needs to be done to determine the effectiveness of llamas as guard animals. Wildlife biologists Knowlton, Gese, and Jaeger, noted that, as of 1999, there have been no systematic field studies of the behavior of coyotes toward guard animals. In fact, they discovered that radio-collared coyotes have been found in close proximity to sheep bedding grounds and an attending guard dog. One hypothesis is that although a guard animal may not force coyotes away from livestock grazing areas, they may change the coyotes' agenda when nearby.

The Iowa study involved 145 sheep producers using guard llamas. Average ranches used one gelded male llama, which was pastured in 250 to 300 acres containing 250 to 300 sheep. Before using guard llamas, an average of 11 percent of the flocks were lost annually. After using llamas, ranchers reported an average loss of 1 percent annually. In dollars, that amounted to an average annual savings of $1,034 for each rancher.

Llamas may be expensive, but fortunately, they have a life span of about 12 to 15 years. For most livestock producers, a llama's longevity will offset its cost. A gelded male llama, which many producers claim will make the best guard llama, should cost you about $800 to $1,000.

Llamas are usually weaned when they are 6 to 8 months of age, and males are usually castrated at 8 to 24 months. The Iowa study indicated that llamas can be placed with sheep at almost any age after weaning. The average age of the llamas they put with sheep was 2 years, but they ranged from a few months to more than 12 years old. In nearly all of the cases, llamas bonded with sheep in only a few days.

When llamas spot a coyote near the livestock, they often run at him with enthusiasm. Once they get near a coyote (if the predator hasn't already headed for the hills), a llama will often kick furiously or sway its head side to side (an aggressive gesture). Guard llamas, however, don't always act this way with other predators. For instance, bears and mountain lions have been sighted among livestock herds where llamas are present. Sometimes the llama will pay little or no attention to larger predators, and allow them to kill livestock. How's that for a protector?

Still, llamas are considered an effective guard animal against several canines, including coyotes, foxes, and dogs. Researchers claim they flat out dislike canines. Their motivation to protect sheep from canines is a tight bond with the sheep.

Sheep producers have used South American llamas in North America since the 1980s. The natural behavior of llamas is to protect territories and family groups. They are also known for their ability to remain alert for long periods of time.

According to an article by Laurie E. Meadows and Frederick F. Knowlton, "Efficacy of Guard Llamas to Reduce Canine Predation on Domestic Sheep," guard llamas provide some advantages over guard dogs:

- greater longevity
- fewer training requirements
- faster acquisition of guardian status
- fewer special management considerations involving food and maintenance
- compatibility with other depredation control techniques

There have been numerous positive testimonies from ranchers and landowners who use guard llamas to protect sheep. Nevertheless, since most of the testimonies are based on interviews and surveys, biologists have gone a step further. Meadows and Knowlton evaluated the effectiveness of llamas to reduce canine predation on domestic sheep by comparing data on sheep lost to predators between flocks with llamas and comparable flocks without llamas. They also conducted surveys to assess producer opinions about guard llama effectiveness.

In 1996 Meadows and Knowlton placed 20 llamas with Utah sheep producers and compared data collected from these flocks over 20 months. This came after the two researchers conducted telephone interviews with sheep producers regarding husbandry and predator control practices. Interested producers were selected to participate in the study of guard llamas if they had a history of sheep loss to coyotes, grazed their sheep year-round in fenced pastures, and were not already using a guard animal. The number of flocks and the number of sheep within the flocks of the selected producers varied considerably.

Researchers telephoned sheep producers every two weeks from May 1996 through December 1997. The numbers of ewes and lambs that died within each two-week period were reported and categorized. Categories of sheep death included predator-caused, natural, accidental, or unknown. If a predator kill occurred, the producer was asked about the number of sheep killed and the predator species responsible. The researchers didn't stop there, however. They also wanted to know the number of sheep in the flock, the size and topography of the pasture, and whether any depredation control methods had been used during the previous two weeks. They asked producers about the llama's behavior, whether they incorporated any changes into their sheep management program because of the llama, and about the llama's interaction with the sheep. During summer and fall, the biologists visited each treatment and control flock more than three times to obtain additional research information.

Sheep producers who participated in the study managed their sheep in various ways. Some pastured their sheep most of the year away from, but in the same valley as, their homes. Others lambed at their farms but moved the flocks to mountain pastures in summer. Only a few producers kept their sheep near their homes year-round. Pasture cover and topography ranged from short grass and flat terrain to densely treed and mountainous areas, with treatment and control flocks dispersed fairly evenly among the various pasture types. Treatment flocks were determined by the number of llamas, with each llama placed with a separate flock in April 1996. Control flocks were those without llamas.

At the study's conclusion, 320 sheep were reported lost to predators, with lambs comprising 85 percent of these losses. Coyotes shared the predation with black bears, mountain lions, red foxes, domestic dogs, and ravens. Nevertheless, canines (coyotes, dogs, and foxes) accounted for 92 percent of all sheep losses to predators reported during the study.

Canine predators killed more sheep and lambs during the first and second summer grazing season than during the winter grazing season. During the first summer treatment flocks lost 42 sheep to predators. During the second summer 35 sheep were lost. Control flocks, however, lost 128 sheep in the first summer and only 32 in the second. During the winter grazing season 10 sheep were lost in treatment flocks and 8 in control flocks. In treatment flocks coyotes killed 63 sheep. In control flocks, they killed 193. Surprisingly, though, dogs killed 22 sheep in treatment flocks but only 10 in control flocks. Similarly, mountain lions killed 16 sheep in treatment flocks and 6 in control flocks. Other predators killed fewer sheep in treatment flocks. Red foxes killed two sheep in treatment flocks and three sheep in control flocks; black bears killed no sheep in treatment flocks and two in control flocks.

So just how effective are guard llamas? Before hearing what the researchers had to say, we'll examine three surveys of the producers, one that occurred before the study, one that took place right after the study, and another one year after the study. Before the study, 12 of 20 (60 percent) of the producers who received llamas claimed "no opinion" on guard llama effectiveness in reducing predation on domestic sheep. None believed that guard llamas would be "very effective." Thirty percent thought guard llamas would be "effective," and 10 percent predicted llamas would be "not effective." Of those producers who had guard llamas with their sheep for 20 months, 9 of 20 (45 percent) claimed the llamas were "very effective" at reducing predation on their sheep. Another 45 percent rated llamas as "effective." None had "no opinion," and two (10 percent) claimed that llamas were "not effective."

By the end of the second summer grazing season, 17 treatment producers were given the option of purchasing their llama. Ninety-four percent paid $350 each, and one with two llamas decided not to purchase either. One year later, researchers noted that 15 producers were still using llamas as guard animals. Of the 15 still using llamas, 53 percent rated them as "very effective." Forty-seven percent rated them as "effective," and none claimed "no opinion" or rated their llamas as "not effective."

Producers of treatment flocks were asked several interesting questions regarding guard llamas, other than how they rated llamas. Most believed their llamas reduced the number of sheep lost to predators and would recommend using guard llamas to

Guard animals, such as llamas, often make aggressive protectors of livestock.

other sheep producers. Producers also said they generally did not have to change their sheep management practices to accommodate the llama. Seventy percent of the producers rated themselves very satisfied with their guard llama, while 20 percent were satisfied, and 10 percent were somewhat satisfied.

Researchers are cautious about relying solely upon opinions of producers when determining the effectiveness of guard llamas to protect sheep. For instance, could the management care of a llama affect their opinion? Would their opinion sway if they actually witnessed a llama harassing a canine? Regardless of these possibilities, most producers who have used llamas as sheep guards appear supportive of their use.

As for what the researchers had to say, they estimated that sheep losses due to predation in treated areas during the first summer grazing season were only about half of those that occurred in areas without llamas. Similar results occurred during the second grazing season. They added that direct assessments of sheep loss and producer opinions suggest that llamas can reduce lamb losses to canine predators. They also recommended that guard llamas be considered part of an integrated depredation control program that includes other nonlethal and lethal depredation control methods when necessary.

Guard Dogs

Many centuries ago guard dogs were used in Europe and Asia to protect livestock. Unfortunately, these folks did not pass along much information about the success and failures of guard dogs. Only recently have researchers discovered a few facts about dogs protecting livestock.

Dogs are effective guard animals, but sometimes they don't work out as well as llamas because of the variability between individual dogs. Researchers have noted that some dogs will protect livestock while others of the same breed may not. With this in mind, let's go ahead and get the bad news about guard dogs out of the way.

Speculation has it that dogs are at a disadvantage when they must guard large herds over vast areas. In addition, rough and dense terrain will affect a dog's ability to guard a herd, and increase the possibility of coyotes stalking. Additionally, livestock producers often find it necessary to train dogs and supervise them carefully. This in itself is a job that not all individuals have the expertise to handle. But an even worse problem may crop up: Rover, if poorly trained and supervised, may decide to kill livestock himself. While running freely, he may also harass and attack wild animals that come near the pastures and livestock he guards. Research also indicates that some guard dogs will harass and sometime attack humans who come near the dog's domain. Another concern is using a supplemental control method such as trapping or shooting. Dogs may hinder the use of these methods.

Nevertheless, guard dogs often protect livestock against predation. They certainly beat the heck out of using no guard animal, particularly when you raise large herds that are difficult to monitor. Are they as effective as guard llamas? That's very hard to determine, but many say yes.

A study on guard dogs, similar to the one on llamas, was conducted by the U.S. Department of Agriculture's Veterinary Service. Of the 38 percent of sheep producers who used guard

dogs, 88 percent said their dogs "moderately" deterred predation or were "very effective" in deterring predation.

The best guard dogs are those that want to protect and stay
with the sheep without harming them. They're intelligent and
alert; the most devoted dogs are those that grew up with the
herd. Nevertheless, don't expect even the most intelligent,
alert, and devoted guard dog to be a herding dog, too. There's a
big difference. Guard dogs are supposed to be a corporate
member of the flock, living with it and following it to any pasture or corral, whereas a herding dog has a natural instinct to
move the flock from Point A to Point B.

Let's look at the differences in breeds of herding dogs and
guard dogs. Most producers agree that the two most popular
species of herding dogs are Australian shepherds and border
collies. Both will bite, bark, and chase sheep when necessary to
move them from one area to another. They rely on signals from
their handler, and usually aren't allowed time alone with the
herd. On the other hand, a guard dog will spend time alone
with the sheep, and it's taboo for him to bite, bark, or chase
sheep. Moreover, he doesn't rely on signals from handlers; instead, he works instinctively.

You can use various breeds of dogs to protect livestock, but
some are better than others. Normally, guard dogs behaviorally
mature slowly. Some do it when they are 18 to 30 months of
age, while others are younger. Some don't mature at all. You
shouldn't expect a young dog to do as well as a mature, experienced dog. Independent behavior is another factor when
choosing a guard dog. Some breeds are selected for their affin-
ity for humans; however, most are traditionally selected for their

ability to act independently in their guarding role. To choose a breed of guard dog, you might want to consider the following research.

According to Jeffrey S. Green and Roger A. Woodruff of USDA Wildlife Services, U.S. dog research was conducted primarily at two locations: at Hampshire College's New England Farm Center (NEFC) in Massachusetts and at the U.S. Sheep Experiment Station (USSES), a USDA Agricultural Research Service facility in Idaho. At the NEFC researchers worked with several breeds of dog from Europe and Asia. They included the Maremma, Planinetz, Anatolian shepherd, and various crosses of these breeds. At the USSES the Komondor, Great Pyrenees, and Akbash species were studied. Other breeds of dog with a history of protecting livestock include the Kuvasz and the Briard. The Navajo used mongrel dogs to protect livestock, although Green and Woodruff noted that these breeds were not the result of a specific breeding program. Their success was probably related to rearing and training.

In the 1986 Idaho study approximately 400 people using livestock guarding dogs were surveyed. There was no difference in the rate of success among breeds, but researchers did note behavioral differences. For instance, a greater number of Komondors bit people than did Great Pyrenees, Akbash, or Anatolians. Fewer Great Pyrenees injured livestock than did Komondors, Akbash, or Anatolians.

Green and Woodruff also reported that Great Pyrenees were rated significantly better than Anatolian shepherds in an evaluation of yearling livestock guarding dogs. Anatolian shepherds were rated lower primarily because of their tendency to injure or kill sheep.

Interestingly, the 1986 Idaho survey noted that most breeds of guard dogs were aggressive to predators and other dogs. Great Pyrenees, though, seemed to be somewhat less aggressive to dogs, but a little more aggressive to other guarding dogs. The two researchers observed a difference in the rate of behavioral maturation in Great Pyrenees and Komondors at the USSES. Great Pyrenees exhibited behavioral maturity at a younger age and seemed to exhibit puppylike behavior less frequently than USSES Komondors. They also noted that Anatolians exhibited a delay in behavioral maturity similar to that of Komondors.

Common Guard Dogs	*Uncommon Guard Dogs*
Akbash (Turkey)	Poodle
Anatolian shepherd (Turkey)	Irish setter
Briard (France)	Chihuahua
Great Pyrenees (France and Spain)	Beagle
Kangal (Turkey)	Dachshund (wiener dog)
Komondor (Hungary)	Collie
Kuvasz (Hungary)	Australian shepherd
Shar Planinetz (Yugoslavia)	Terrier
Maremma (Italy)	Schnauzer

Two guarding dogs have received strong recognition in recent years—the Akbash and Kangal. David and Judith Nelson claim responsibility for introducing the Akbash dog breed to North America in the late 1970s. Together, they have worked hard to promote the breed and its natural livestock guardian instincts. Rightfully so, because there have been many testimonies regarding the Akbash dog's success in protecting livestock. The Nelsons recently imported and established the Kangal dog, another Turkish animal that is becoming a significant livestock guard dog. The Kangal has proved itself for many years in Turkey.

It's recommended you purchase a guard dog from a reputable breeder who knows the dog he or she sells. Some breeders offer various guarantees on their dogs, including a replacement if an animal fails to perform as expected. For more information on guard dog breeds, and for purchasing information, see chapter 12.

Does it make good economic sense to use a guard dog? First, consider annual predation and cost. Second, consider the cost of the dog. Purchase prices vary according to breed, bloodline, age, and breeder. For the studies, the USDA purchased 100 guard dogs, seven to eight weeks old, of various breeds during 1987 and 1988 at an average price (including air freight to Idaho) of $443 per dog. Of the dogs they purchased, Great Pyrenees were the most readily available and generally cost less than other breeds.

A 1986 survey by the USDA showed that 82 percent of 400 producers with guarding dogs reported that the dogs represented an economic asset. Nine percent claimed they broke even, and 9 percent said they considered the dogs an economic liability. Consider both the benefits and problems listed in this table.

Benefits and Problems of Guard Dogs*

Benefits

Reduced predation

Reduced labor (corralling, monitoring, etc.)

Protection for family members and farm property

Peace of mind

Increased utilization of acres where predators made grazing prohibitive before using dogs

Improved potential for profit

Increased self-reliance in managing predator problems

Dog alerts owner to disturbance (predators) near the flock

If night confinement is discontinued, pastures can be more efficiently utilized and condition of sheep may improve

Problems

Dog does not guard sheep

Dog harasses sheep (usually a play behavior), resulting in injury or death

Expenditure of labor to train and supervise the dog

Dog is aggressive to people

Dog destroys property (chewing objects and digging)

Dog is subject to illness, injury, or premature death

Dog roams beyond farm boundaries, causing problems with neighbors

Dog interferes when sheep are moved or interferes with herd dog

Dog affects the use of other predator control activities

*As reported by researchers Green and Woodruff.

Green and Woodruff saw no difference between the success rates of male and female guard dogs; thus, choosing the sex of a dog becomes a personal preference. Some producers do recommend that you spay or neuter the dog. They say it's best to spay females at about six months of age and neuter males at about nine months of age.

How many dogs should you purchase? Green and Woodruff found that an experienced dog may effectively patrol several hundred acres containing hundreds of sheep, while younger dogs might not. Of course, consider also the types and numbers of predators, and the habitat. A single dog may cover flat, open areas, but you may need several dogs to cover a dense area. Keep in mind, too, that multiple dogs may fight.

Producers suggest you bring a future guard dog home at seven to eight weeks of age. Isolate the pup in a confinement with three to six sheep (preferably lambs), making certain he cannot escape. The pup should be checked several times a day. Although you can pet him, make sure you don't overdo it, since this could hinder the dog's bonding with the sheep. The socialization period should last for about 8 weeks, until the pup is about 16 weeks old. Then you can release him into a larger pasture area with the flock. Obedience training should be initiated in the first days of the pup's introduction into the flock; however, excessive training may strengthen the bond between you and the dog and weaken the dog's bond with the sheep.

As the dog gains guarding experience, he may display certain behaviors, such as barking, scent marking, and patrolling more or less often. If coyotes frequently visit the pasture, a dog may mark and patrol more than he would if they didn't. Guard dogs rarely bark.

Don't think that all your problems will end once you rush out and buy a guard dog. It could happen, but don't take it for granted. The dog might not provide any benefits. He might not be as aggressive or protective as necessary, or be able to pick up the training methods you apply. Perhaps the training will become too much for you to handle. You must realize that you can't turn a guard dog on and off at will. They usually work at their pace, not at yours. Many guard dogs are slow to mature, and in some cases, it could take them two years to learn to do their jobs properly. Nevertheless, if they remain healthy and all else goes well, they can give you years of good service at an unbeatable price.

Guard Donkeys

For some inexplicable reason, donkeys hate canines. This was first noted years ago when observers saw how they reacted to dogs. Coyotes can also expect to elicit a strong dislike when they meet up with a donkey in the middle of livestock. When a donkey sees a coyote coming near, he expresses aggression: He'll show his teeth, bray (*hee-haw*), kick, and often run toward the predator. In some cases, he may even bite the coyote. Donkeys often display aggression to foxes and bobcats, too, but sometimes they themselves will become prey if they get near wolves, bears, and mountain lions.

As with any guard animal, pros and cons exist. For instance, donkeys are easy to maintain, since they will graze with livestock. Nevertheless, donkeys should not be allowed to eat feed with anabolic agents (Rumensin and Bovatec) containing additives intended only for ruminants. They also have a life span of 10 to 15 years. Surprisingly, a donkey might cost less than a young guard dog with no experience. You can expect to pay about $150 to $200 for a donkey, although you must also add in the cost of annual health care, such as worming and vaccinations. You may also need to have the donkey's hooves trimmed periodically. If you use another coyote control method, such as a leghold trap, note that a donkey is less likely to be injured in the trap than a guard dog.

The success of donkeys as guard animals is variable. A Texas survey indicated that some owners of donkeys had success, but many said they did not make effective guard animals. Nova Scotia sheep owners had split opinions about their effectiveness.

Although producers use guard donkeys primarily for protecting sheep, the Missouri Department of Conservation reported that goat and hog producers also use them. Hog producers have found they offer some protection to sows giving birth in the woods.

Most livestock producers prefer to use geldings and jennies for guarding. Even if you have a jenny guarding your flock, however, consider that she might not work as hard on some days as she does on others. For example, if she has a foal, she'll care less about the flock than it. In addition, when her time comes to breed, she'll be more interested in looking for a handsome donkey than chasing away a coyote.

You won't need to provide training for guard donkeys, but like other guard animals, they must bond with livestock to make certain they stay with the herd. Keep in mind the following suggestions when deciding whether guard donkeys are for you:

- Select only medium to large stock (never miniatures).
- Raise donkeys with the animals they will guard.

- Geldings and jennies make the best guards since jacks (males) may be overly protective and too aggressive to livestock.
- Use only one donkey per pasture; two or more will seek the company of each other.
- Test guarding capabilities by placing a dog in the pasture, and be prepared to reject a donkey that doesn't show aggression to the canine.
- Use the donkey in a pasture less than 600 acres containing no more than 200 sheep.

Using a guard animal to protect your livestock could be an expensive investment. Nonetheless, if the animal performs as you hope, more than likely it will save you money in the end. Before making the investment, calculate your annual losses and compare them to the costs of obtaining and maintaining a guard animal. If it seems a guard animal could save you money, go for it with the idea that it's a test. Some guard animals work, and others don't. But keep in mind, research indicates that using a guard animal is probably an easier form of controlling coyotes than any lethal method, and perhaps even more effective.

10

Supplemental Livestock Protection

QUESTION: *What are some of the good things about coyotes?*

ANSWER: *They are cute and they will eat a lot of rabbits.*
—Allyson Harlowe, age 12

C oyotes do enjoy the taste of rabbit, and they will eat their share of them when available. A surplus of rabbits might also prevent coyotes from killing livestock and poultry. Unfortunately, although female rabbits have several litters a year that keep North America's coyotes well supplied with prey, it's not enough to satisfy Wily and his predatory friends. Most rabbits (80 percent) don't stick around long enough to celebrate their first birthday, and not just because coyotes snatch them up. Instead, nature controls rabbit populations through cold and wet conditions, and makes them available to numerous species of predators. We also assist in the control of rabbits, thanks to a few hunters and the invention of automobiles.

Livestock is prey to a coyote, as are rabbits and several other rodents. Livestock losses account for millions of dollars in damages annually. That's not to say that everyone who raises livestock will suffer losses. On the contrary, some livestock producers don't have to worry about coyotes preying upon livestock. There are two primary reasons for this: The producers use control methods, or the density of coyotes in their area is low.

Livestock damage due to coyotes isn't limited to large producers of sheep, cattle, hogs, and goats. Small-time producers also suffer losses. They range from folks who raise only a few chickens to those who have a goat or two in the yard to keep the area free of weeds (as well as all other green and growing things).

Various factors influence coyote depredation of livestock. According to researchers Knowlton, Gese, and Jaeger, sheep producers find that the breed of sheep, sheep management practices, coyote behavior, environmental factors, and depredation management programs are factors that determine how many sheep are lost to coyotes. They pointed out that the vulnerability of livestock is dependent upon several factors, too, including sociality, grazing dispersion, attentiveness, and maternal protection.

However, Knowlton, Gese, and Jaeger added that protecting livestock from coyote depredation is a complex endeavor, with each case frequently requiring an assessment of its unique legal, social, economic, biological, and technical aspects. Successful resolution of wildlife conflicts involves the efficiency of various management approaches, including both corrective and preventive techniques.

There are a variety of control methods you can use to protect livestock from coyotes, from predator fences and guard animals to various husbandry practices. Nevertheless, not all methods of control are 100 percent effective. Of the numerous nonremoval control techniques that have been used to create physical barriers between coyotes and livestock or to deter coyotes from attacking livestock, a significant number fail. It's best to start at the top with husbandry practices, and work our way through various other control methods.

Livestock Husbandry

Livestock husbandry is actually the practice of breeding and raising livestock with careful herd management. Although this section will focus primarily on sheep, these husbandry practices apply to other livestock. Knowlton, Gese, and Jaeger list six preventive husbandry practices:

1. confining or concentrating flocks during periods of vulnerability (at night or during lambing)
2. using herders
3. shed lambing
4. removing livestock carrion from pastures to retard food recognition by coyotes
5. synchronizing birthing to reduce the period of maximum vulnerability
6. keeping young animals in areas with little cover and in close proximity to humans

These husbandry practices are somewhat self-explanatory; however, you should note that they normally require additional effort, and may only delay the onset of predation. To give you an example, penning animals at night requires additional effort and frequently creates spot deterioration of pastures. Shed lambing decreases mortality but requires additional labor as well as a ready and affordable supply of feed. Keeping young animals confined and close to humans means producers must provide cover and protection.

Since coyote predation typically follows a seasonal pattern (most losses occur in spring and summer, when coyotes must feed their young), many livestock producers change the lambing season to fall. Kansas livestock growers have reported positive results by postponing the time in which livestock raise their young.

Moving livestock to new and safer grazing areas should also help avert predation. For instance, when lambing occurs you should put your sheep in open pastures where they can readily spot predators. Thick grazing areas, those with dense vegetation and large rocks, make it easier for a coyote to sneak up on livestock. Coyotes also find it easier to prey on livestock if ravines and streams are present, laying up in these areas and, while staying cool and rested, waiting for livestock to come in for shade and water.

Since carrion offers a free meal that attracts coyotes and, often, many other scavengers that also invite coyotes, always check grazing areas daily for dead livestock. If a coyote hasn't been killing livestock, it may begin to once it discovers a carcass. Always bury the carcass away from pastures where livestock spend most of their time.

A study in Canada showed that coyotes often depend upon winter carrion for survival in livestock-raising areas; however, when the carrion was scrupulously removed in winter, coyotes moved away. Another study in the western states found that sheep producers who hauled away or buried sheep carcasses had 40 to 50 percent fewer losses than producers who left carcasses in pastures.

All carrion attracts coyotes, but dead pigs seem to bring them running. An Illinois study showed that 12 of 46 swine producers who did not properly dispose of dead swine had coyote problems, compared to only 1 of 34 producers who immediately removed or buried dead animals.

One exception to removing carrion occurs if you want to remove a predating coyote. Livestock producers use carrion as bait to lure in and identify a problem coyote. The following chapter will discuss baiting coyotes in more detail.

If it's impossible to confine vulnerable livestock, consider using shepherds. Herders have been used for thousands of years to protect livestock, and they still work today. Regardless of whether you ride a horse or simply spend time with your livestock, a coyote will fear you. Many herders also carry a firearm and are able to dispose of coyotes when they see them. Cost, however, must be considered when using humans as shepherds.

Sick and injured livestock should be removed from the rest of the herd immediately. Several studies have indicated that handicapped livestock attract coyotes. Coyotes don't feed on the weak only, but they are easy targets, so coyotes will usually pick on diseased or injured animals before they attack a healthy individual. Unfortunately, if they feed upon two or three weak animals, they turn to the healthy ones as soon as the easier prey is no longer available.

Confining livestock close to humans at night is an effective method of controlling predation, because coyotes don't usually approach residences. Exceptions do exist in some areas where coyotes are used to people. Nevertheless, confinement is an option that should be considered if you can't afford proper fencing or guard animals. If you combine frightening devices with confinement, the results are often spectacular. After a while, some livestock, particularly sheep, may not require that you move them into confinement. Sheep learn quickly that confinement offers the best chance of survival. They also prefer the overhead cover when cold, wet, windy weather prevails. Effort may be necessary at first to direct them into a barnyard or building at night, but after a few trips your livestock will get the idea and move on their own. Some livestock producers use confinement techniques after predation begins. While the animals are confined, you can then attempt control methods, such as shooting or trapping a problem coyote (if legal).

Confinement practices sound promising, but they do have drawbacks. Anytime you confine animals into a small area, you

Livestock, such as sheep, adjust quickly to moving from pasture to shelter.

should be concerned about parasites and manure concentration. Nevertheless, you can medicate your livestock for parasites, and you should clean up manure after each night of confinement. You should also know that your livestock will have less time to graze when confined; supplemental feeding may be necessary. Sheep raisers may also find that the quality of wool decreases when animals are confined.

Also, consider "shed lambing" as a husbandry practice. Shed lambing is just what it implies: You arrange for livestock to be born in a shed. Of course, this could be any building, or perhaps a small fenced area. Shed lambing protects newborns from being snatched by coyotes soon after they're born. This form of predation has victimized cattle, hogs, goats, and sheep, and has probably occurred during the birthing process of many game animals, too. Most cattle predation occurs when calves are less than one week old. If cows are left to give birth in pastures, they often select secluded locations attractive to coyotes. Wily sits back and waits for the animal to be born, but after Mom gets the job done, he rushes in to enjoy an easy meal. Shed lambing can be costly for producers, because it may require special care of livestock and the construction of fences or barns, but these costs may be offset by an increase in young livestock.

You also can consider combining livestock. In other words, you can place sheep with cattle, or cattle with goats. When a coyote approaches a sheep or goat, the cattle often encircle the vulnerable animal. When this occurs, the coyote has second thoughts about attacking.

When it comes to cows, you should note that Hereford calves are most vulnerable to predation. A Hereford mother tends to leave her calf behind when she heads for food and water. However, longhorn calves will travel with their mothers when they move.

Frightening Devices

There are several types of frightening devices you can use to protect livestock from coyotes. Most periodically emit bursts of light or sound. You can use these in open pastures and inside or near confinement areas. You might not be able to use some frightening devices, because neighbors usually frown on the idea of their houses being lit up like Christmas trees every night, or sirens going off when they are enjoying a sweet dream.

You should also note that frightening devices might not always be effective. Many do scare away coyotes, but only for a few nights. Coyotes will soon figure out that frightening devices are, well, only frightening devices. They scare, but they never hurt. When using frightening devices, they will be most effective if you use them in large numbers. You've heard the old saying, "One's enough, two's too many, and three's a crowd." When it comes to frightening devices to scare away coyotes, one's not enough, two's not many, and three's best.

The more often you move the devices, the more they'll scare away coyotes. In other words, keep Wily guessing. When he comes into an area where frightening devices have scared him previously, he'll expect them to do their thing right where they did it before. But if you move the devices to new locations, you can say what Gomer Pyle commonly said: "Surprise, surprise."

Here's a list of frightening devices that might raise the hairs on a coyote's back and bring your neighbor over for a chat in the middle of the night.

- **Propane exploders:** These rascals bang like a gunshot and may send a coyote into a dead run. You can set propane exploders, sometimes called propane cannons, to go off at random intervals, but they're most effective when they fire at short intervals about 15 minutes apart. A propane exploder costs about $300. Maintenance may occasionally be necessary, and the exploder might not fire when it rains. Coyotes, and any other animals in the area, will get used to the exploders very quickly. For instance, while deer hunting in southern Illinois near several oil wells, I noticed that they repeatedly backfired. These explosions were loud enough to pass for a shotgun blast. Yet deer often fed in fields only a few yards from the oil wells, and didn't blink an eye when they exploded.

- **Radios and music:** Livestock producers have discovered that a radio playing all night long will deter coyotes, at least temporarily. Both vehicle and tractor radios are commonly used. Transistor radios may work, too, but only if you keep a supply of fresh batteries on hand. For the best results, move the radio every day or two. Since voices seem to work better than relaxing music, you could consider using a cassette. In fact, you could record the cassette yourself and use one of the following messages:
  A. Get out of here you good-for-nothing . . .
  B. I'll blow your dirty brains out if you don't . . .
  C. Don't you dare bite that little lamb . . .
  D. If you wanna kill poor little innocent animals, head on over the hill to Joe's place.

- **Lighting:** Studies have shown that nighttime lighting will help reduce livestock predation. In Kansas a study of 100 sheep producers showed that using lights above corrals at night had positive results. Of 79 sheep killed by coyotes in corrals, only 3 were killed in corrals with lights. Those with electric-eye sensors that turn on at dusk and off at dawn are best. Floodlights are also used. Nevertheless, don't count on spectacular results when using lights as frightening devices, unless your livestock is confined close to your residence. You might increase the effectiveness of lights by using revolving or flashing devices. One good thing about using lights close to your residence is that they enable you to see what goes on near the corral. If so, you might be able to sneak up on and destroy the coyote causing damage.

- **Sirens:** Portable sirens and the Electronic Guard are similar, since both are noisemakers. Both may scare off coyotes for a while, and both will drive you and your neighbors crazy. The good news is they also may keep criminals from hiding out nearby. The Electronic Guard is usually preferred over portable sirens. The USDA developed the standard Electronic Guard. It's battery operated and consists of a strobe light and siren controlled by a variable interval timer that's activated at night with a photoelectric cell. It has been fairly effective in scaring coyotes. Kansas officials reported that many cattle producers have seen positive results, but most of the users are sheep producers. The cost of the Electronic Guard is about $250. The number you need depends upon the size of the pasture and the amount of existing cover. If there's minimal cover, assume you'll need one Electronic Guard per 15 acres of pasture. Like other frightening devices, you should move them every couple of days to a new location.

- **Bells:** Your neighbor will love your decision to place bells around the necks of your livestock instead of using sirens, propane exploders, and lights. Your livestock might love it, too. On the other hand, coyotes will probably hate the bells. A Kansas study found that coyotes attacked no sheep that wore bells. Nobody knows for sure why simple bells reduced predation, but some believe that they sounded so strange and unusual that coyotes were too afraid to approach livestock.

Various types of frightening devices are available from farm implement stores and mail-order catalogs. If you can't locate a particular device, contact your local animal damage control agency or the USDA office closest to you.

Electronic Dog-Training Collars

Although most livestock producers would not associate electronic dog-training collars with protecting livestock and deterring predation, research indicates positive results.

In 1997, to test the effectiveness of an electronic dog-training collar, William F. Andelt, Robert L. Phillips, Kenneth S. Gruver, and Jerry W. Guthrie transported 20 rambouillet lambs to the National Wildlife Research Center's Predator Research Facility near Logan, Utah, where captive coyotes had been fitted with electronic collars. Their intention was to deter the coyotes placed with the sheep from attacking during a 22-week period. The test collars were set on the highest power setting on a radio transmitter, which resulted in 325 pulses per second of 600 to 640 volts. In each attack case, the researchers shocked the collared coyote.

The researchers later reported that five coyotes attempted 13 attacks on lambs. All 13 attempts were averted when the coyotes were shocked with the collars. Officials also noted that the probability of subsequent attempted attacks was greatly reduced, which led to coyotes avoiding and retreating from lambs for more than four months.

The coyotes appeared quick to associate the shocks with the lambs they attacked, and most coyotes interrupted their attack immediately upon the administered shock. The four researchers concluded that the use of collars on livestock has the potential to reduce coyote predation on domestic sheep in limited areas and offer protection from other carnivore predation on domestic or endangered species.

While this may sound promising, the researchers said that electronic training collars would only have limited applications, and their high cost may be prohibitive. They called for further field testing to prove their value. Whether electronic dog collars will ever become a feasible method for controlling livestock predation remains a question.

Livestock Protection Collars

Livestock protection collars (LPCs) should not be confused with electronic dog-training collars. Introduced in the 1970s, collars with two rupturable bladders filled with Compound 1080 are placed around a prey animal's neck. Since most coyotes attack livestock at the throat, they will rupture the bladders and swallow the Compound 1080. Officials claim that when the coyote receives a lethal dose of 1080, he will die a painless death within a few hours.

One advantage of LPCs is that they kill only targeted coyotes. Shooting and trapping coyotes may remove predators that aren't killing livestock. LPCs also eliminate coyotes that have attacked livestock but have managed to elude other predation control methods.

Researchers determined that LPCs are most effective when used on smaller animals (25 to 50 pounds). Since the collar doesn't adequately cover the neck and throat of larger animals, some coyotes may not rupture the compartment that contains Compound 1080. In a study of six ranches in Idaho and Montana, only 18 of 34 small collars were bitten by coyotes in attacks on collared lambs that weighed about 70 pounds each.

Tests have been conducted on larger collars containing a higher dose of Compound 1080. Richard J. Burns, Doris E. Zemlicka, and Peter J. Savarie tested the effectiveness of LLPCs (large livestock protection collars) in 1991 and 1992 at the Denver Wildlife Research Center's Predator Research Site in Millville, Utah. The LLPCs, designed for goats and sheep, contained the same formulation of Compound 1080 as the smaller LPCs. According to the researchers, during 32 pen tests involving 19 large sheep wearing LLPCs, 12 adult coyotes made 14 neck or throat attacks. In 10 of these attacks (71 percent), LLPCs were punctured, and all 10 coyotes died. These coyotes showed signs of intoxication in an average of 203 minutes, succumbing 93 minutes later. The researchers also noted that the average length of time from attack to death did not differ between the groups of coyotes that punctured one collar compartment and the ones that punctured two. The team concluded that LLPCs were more effective in deterring coyote predation on large sheep than the previously registered LPCs.

Although Compound 1080 had been banned in 1972, the LPC containing the poison was approved by the U.S. Environmental Protection Agency in 1989, primarily with the intention of protecting goats and sheep from depredation. However, LPCs are not an option for most livestock producers. Only those ranchers with approved training and accountability programs in a few states—Montana, New Mexico, South Dakota, Texas, and Wyoming—can use LPCs.

M-44 Ejectors

Like LPCs, the M-44 ejector is designed to kill coyotes preying on livestock. It works by ejecting sodium cyanide powder into the mouth of the coyote when the attack occurs. When the animal pulls on a baited M-44, the ejector fires the powder. Death occurs quickly, usually within two minutes after the device is triggered.

According to the USDA, the M-44 is safe to use. If the contents of the cyanide capsule spill onto the ground, the ingredient turns to gas and dissipates once it encounters soil moisture. If no moisture is present, the powder filters through the soil, where microorganisms degrade it. Research also indicates that the toxic effects of the cyanide are short lived because it decomposes into a harmless substance within 24 hours. Nevertheless, anyone using an M-44 is required to carry an antidote kit.

The M-44 is registered by the Environmental Protection Agency and can be used only by trained and certified applicators. When used, trained personnel check them at least once a week.

Repellents

Currently, you cannot purchase a commercial repellent that will deter or stop coyote predation of livestock, although researchers have tested a variety of products. Some of these, particularly those that include quinine hydrochloride and capsaicin, show promise; however, researchers have provided evidence that predation has continued even when these repellents were used.

A number of animal scents act as repellents and deter herbivores, such as deer. Unfortunately, they're the scents of predators. Coyote and fox scent powder and urine are often used. And while coyote scent may deter foxes, fox scent won't deter coyotes.

One reason repellents don't work is that coyotes primarily rely on visual cues when stalking and preparing to attack. Their senses of taste and smell seem to have little bearing on their desire to go ahead with an attack. For this reason, some animals that were sprayed with repellents have been killed by coyotes, but not devoured.

Fencing

Various types of fences will prevent coyotes from attacking livestock; however, as mentioned in a previous chapter, there is really no such thing as a coyote-proof fence. Coyotes, particularly those that have already enjoyed the taste of livestock, are persistent and will try everything imaginable to get to their prey. They learn to dig under, jump over, and go through a typical livestock fence if an opportunity exists.

As are most other protection and control methods, fences are costly. In the case of large pastures, effective fences probably aren't even feasible—although for small areas, such as night corrals or even day corrals used to protect a few animals, the right fence might suffice, and possibly fit within the budget of many producers.

You can choose to construct an electric, net-wire, or electric *and* net-wire fence. There isn't much cost difference between the two types, but the simple construction of an electric fence usually costs less than a net-wire fence. A net-wire fence is simply a taller fence made of tightly woven wire with small openings. Whichever type you decide on, it will help protect your livestock from predation if constructed properly.

The U.S. Fish and Wildlife Service conducted a survey that summarized sheep losses on 14 farms before and after the installation of electric fences. Prior to fencing, 1,064 sheep were lost during a period of 271 months and 27 lambing seasons. After the fences were installed, and 228 months and 22 lambing seasons passed, only 52 sheep were counted lost. The reduction in predation amounted to 90 percent.

Nova Scotia did a similar study in 1990. They classified fence types as "not electric," "poor electric," and "fair-to-good electric." Those who had fences that were not electric reported an average of 5.1 sheep lost per year, while those with poor electric fences lost an average of 5.5 sheep per year. Individuals with fair-to-good electric fences had an average annual sheep loss of 0.9.

A well-made electric fence should be constructed of smooth, high-tensile wire stretched tightly to a tension of 200 to 300 pounds. Use at least 6 to 12 strands of 12-gauge high-tensile wire, spaced about 6 inches apart. Increasing the number of strands increases the protection the fence will offer your livestock. Adequate bracing at corners is required.

The bottom wire should be barely above the ground. This will prevent a coyote from digging under the bottom wire. The ground below the bottom wire should also be clean to make certain the fence will work. Keep weeds and grass cut close to the ground, and make certain debris is removed and kept away from the wire.

Since the coyote has long and sometimes thick fur, it's suggested you use a minimum charge of 2,000 volts; 4,000 volts is better yet. The higher voltage usually sends a coyote running away and not looking for another way to get inside the fence.

A net-wire fence must be taller than an electric fence. The coyote's first reaction is to go under a fence, and sometimes through it. Since a net-wire fence won't cause the coyote pain when he pushes against bottom or middle, it must be tall enough to keep him from going over. You must also design the fence so the coyote can't go under.

As mentioned previously, the net-wire fence should have small openings, preferably less than 6 inches wide. Four inches or less is even better. The fence should be 5½ to 6 feet high and should be stretched tight and have solid anchors on the corners. A barrier at the bottom and the top will prevent coyotes from going under or over. The barrier at the top should be 1 to 2 feet wide, and slant away from the pen at a 45-degree angle. You can use the same net-wire fencing for the top barrier that you used to construct the fence. The bottom barrier needn't be angled. Again, you can use the same net-wire fencing, running it straight into the ground at least 18 to 24 inches.

Net-wire fences may help you to trap problem coyotes. If trapping is allowed in your area, try setting a trap near the edge of the fence. When a coyote arrives on the scene and discovers that he can't get inside the fence, he'll probably walk the perimeter of the fence looking for an easy way in. Thus, he's sure to run into your trap.

The closest you will get to a coyote-proof fence—and the most expensive fence—is the net-wire and electric fence combination. Follow the instructions for building a net-wire fence, then simply add electric strands to the outside of the existing net wire. About 8 inches away from the net-wire fence, add a high-tensile wire about 6 inches above the ground. This stops coyotes from attempting to dig under the fence. Add another charged wire about 4 to 6 inches above the top of the net-wire fence, ideally a few inches away from the top of the net wire. This will form the top barrier. Use the same voltage I recommended previously—2,000 to 4,000 volts. You can also place a maze of hot wires around your net-wire fence.

Your final option is a portable electric fence. This consists of thin strands of wire running through polyethylene twine or ribbon, commonly called "polytape." You can buy polytape in wire rolls or as a mesh fence in different heights. The benefit of using a portable electric fence is that it can be set up quickly as a temporary holding pen or a corral partition. The downside is that this fence isn't as strong as the others. Livestock hitting against the fence could damage it, leaving them open to predation.

Protecting Fowl and Small Mammals

In this section, I will attempt to pass along a few helpful tips for protecting poultry and other small animals. However, be aware that many other predators prey upon these animals besides coyotes.

Scarecrows alone don't scare away coyotes; however, sweaty clothing on a scarecrow, or perhaps strung out here and there near the fowl and animals you want to protect, may scare them away. You can also scatter sweaty clothes along the boundaries of a pen or housing area. I have often draped a sweaty shirt over a game animal to protect it overnight from coyotes. I've never had a coyote tear into a game animal that was covered with clothing loaded with human scent, although I have seen several game animals that have been ripped apart by coyotes when there was no human smell to deter the predator.

You can try to deter coyotes by using some of the frightening devices mentioned previously. Of course, most lights and sirens offer only temporary relief. You can also leave a radio playing in the area where you house your poultry or animals. Some say hard rock music works best, but I prefer to tranquilize animals and poultry with country-western music.

Chickens and other fowl have sharp eyesight and an instinct to watch for predators. Make sure your fowl can take advantage of their natural defenses by removing all thick brush and debris so that they can spot a predator when he approaches.

Since most attacks occur at night, you must rely on prevention tactics that will keep coyotes away from your poultry and other animals. Some folks believe there's nothing better to protect chickens than a chicken-wire fence. In fact, no chicken-wire fencing will protect poultry against coyotes unless you provide additional barriers under the ground and at the top. For better ideas, read the previous section on fencing.

If you keep fowl in a fenced pen, you may even want to keep a fenced roof over their heads. If you house them at night, make sure there are no openings in their shelter that a coyote could squeeze through. A 6-inch opening is too wide.

If you have a dog that can be trusted with fowl (they are few and far between), consider allowing him to stay in the pen with them. Naturally, if your dog isn't trustworthy, he could kill all your fowl in a short time. Some folks have trained dogs to guard their fowl and other animals. I suppose it's possible, but like dogs that guard sheep and goats, you might need to raise them with the poultry and animals you want to protect. The dogs may form a bond with them and have a natural instinct to protect.

Some fowl, if given an opportunity, will roost in trees and on shelves. I know one man who lost every chicken except one rooster to predators (coyotes were responsible for some of the losses) during the dark hours. For the last two years, that rooster has roosted in a tree. However, fowl that roost in trees are still vulnerable to predation from owls and raccoons.

I suggest that you keep small animals such as rabbits in small enclosures or cages made of hardware cloth. Hardware cloth is stout and has small openings that only a field mouse can squeeze through. However, make certain the bottom of the animal's pen is solid. If it has a wire bottom and sits above the ground, your animal could be in trouble.

Negative responses to using lethal methods of control are understandable, considering they often prove counterproductive, resulting in expanding coyote populations and increasing livestock damage. Researchers and livestock producers have only just begun to test preventive and nonlethal control measures, but we're sure to learn more about livestock protection in the years ahead. Nonetheless, this doesn't necessarily mean that their findings will change the way we do things. On the contrary, with the exception of using guard animals, there may be no better nonlethal control methods or preventive techniques than those mentioned in this chapter.

11

Hunting and Trapping

QUESTION: What would you do if you saw a coyote coming toward you?

ANSWER: I would run because I'm afraid of them.
    —Allyson Harlowe, age 12

lthough a number of control methods mentioned previously in this book may stop coyotes from causing damage or preying on livestock, pets, poultry, and other animals, most of the nonlethal techniques I've discussed only delay the inevitable. Some troublesome coyotes will continue to cause damage despite control methods until they're permanently stopped. Not every problem coyote needs to be killed; however, hunting and trapping are often effective means of eliminating the truly vexatious ones. And while it's true that another coyote may move in and take over where the first left off, shooting or trapping a problem predator may grant permanent or long-term relief.

If you decide to hunt or trap a coyote, check the regulations in your state or province. Keep in mind, too, that county or city ordinances may apply that will overrule state or provincial regulations. The use of certain types of traps or firearms may be banned. Season dates may also be specified. In some cases, a conservation officer or local agency may overrule the usual regulations, depending upon the damage inflicted by a troublesome coyote.

Before getting into hunting and trapping techniques, you should understand that some folks will have a better chance of success than others. Hunting and trapping are arts, perfected by years of experience. That's not to say your first attempt won't be successful; however, the odds of success aren't in your favor. If you don't have previous experience, seek help from someone who does. Throughout this chapter, though, you'll discover several useful hunting and trapping tips that will assist you regardless of previous experience.

Even an experienced hunter or trapper will have a difficult time eliminating several coyotes in a given area; however, it is possible to eliminate one troublesome coyote. In fact, you should base your entire effort on the following imperative: Go after the predator that's causing the damage.

Hunting with Calls

Most hunters rely on distress calls of other animals to lure a coyote into range. Wily may come in running, or he may sneak in. Most of the time, he won't come in at all, but that's precisely why most coyote hunters don't give up the chase. It could be the coyote didn't hear the call; or perhaps he picked up the scent of the hunter, or spotted the hunter before the hunter saw him.

Coyotes are primarily nocturnal, but they're occasionally spotted during midday. The chance of a coyote coming to a call is usually higher at night; he just may be lured in during the first hour of dawn or the last hour of the evening. Some areas allow you to hunt at night with the use of a light.

Camouflage is necessary when you hunt during daylight hours. Experienced hunters rely on total camouflage, right down to their faces and hands. Keep in mind, when using a call, that you are the hunted and the coyote the hunter. He'll be looking for movement and any stationary object that he can identify as prey.

Your setup is vital to success. Before using the call, select a place to sit on the ground. By sitting against a tree, or in brush, you'll blend with the natural habitat. You needn't set up in the precise location where damage has occurred, but you certainly

Hunters should wear camouflage and hide in cover to keep from being spotted by the sharp eyes of an approaching coyote.

don't want to be far from it. Visibility is an essential factor. You must see the coyote before he sees you. In the western plains visibility is seldom a problem; however, since the coyote has expanded his range into dense areas across North America, some hunters have found it more difficult to choose a setup that offers ample visibility. If you're close to agricultural fields, set up along the fringe, or perhaps in a ditch or thicket in the middle of the field.

Always consider wind direction when choosing a setup. The coyote has an excellent sense of smell, and although he may not come in with the wind in his nose, he will surely detect your scent if he does. For this reason, determine from where the coyote will most likely come and set up accordingly.

The effective shooting range of your firearm will also play a role in your setup. A .22-caliber rifle's effective range is limited to about 75 yards or less. Most hunters prefer larger centerfire rifles such as a .22-250 or .243 caliber. These two rifles will increase your shooting range by another 100 yards or more. With a bigger-caliber rifle, the weight of the projectile also increases, enhancing the possibility of making a killing shot. Some hunters prefer 12-gauge shotguns—preferably a 3-inch magnum or larger—accompanied by a heavy load of No. 4 shot or larger. Hunters in dense areas with limited visibility typically use shotguns. Although any shotgun may pattern effectively, today's turkey shotguns, accompanied by an extra-full choke to ensure a tight pattern, are an excellent choice if you assume a 40-yard shot or less. To ensure a quick clean kill, shoot for the head, or on or just behind the shoulder to take out the lungs and heart of the coyote.

Most hunters rely on rabbit distress calls to lure a coyote into range. Some use handheld calls, while others prefer electronic devices (where legal). Handheld calls are easy to operate and require little practice. Electronic devices often use a prerecorded tape of the distress cries of a rabbit or other animal. Although rabbit squeals usually work best, hunters have also had positive results imitating distress sounds of mice, birds, and foxes. Some also use coyote howlers. Handheld howlers are more difficult to master than handheld distress calls, but they often locate coyotes. A few hunters claim they bring in coyotes, but many use them simply to make a coyote howl. Once they locate him, they move in and attempt to lure him in with a distress call.

Using a handheld call allows you to regulate calling intervals. For instance, you can decide when and when not to call, and regulate the volume as necessary. Sometimes a coyote may be close, and you would prefer to decrease the volume of the call—or decide to make no sound at all.

When you begin calling, low volume is usually best in case a coyote is close. After calling for a minute or two, you should spend the next 15 or 20 minutes watching for an approaching coyote. If none shows, increase the volume and call more frequently. This may attract a coyote that did not hear your first calls. Naturally, wind will affect the hearing range of the coyote, as will heavy timber and dense brush. On a still morning or evening, your sound will carry better from a hill than it will from a valley.

If a coyote doesn't come to your call after you increase the volume and call more frequently, try moving 200 yards and starting over, using the same routine mentioned previously.

If a coyote comes in but remains out of range, first give him the opportunity to move closer without enticing him with more calls. Some coyotes will come in only part of the way and stop. After a few minutes, the coyote may decide to come closer. If not, call again, but keep the volume low.

Remote hunting at night with a light works best with two hunters. One can call while the other keeps the light moving, searching out the eyes of a coyote as he approaches. If you hunt at night, you'll want a rechargeable light that offers candlepower of 500,000 or more. Some lights also offer an optional pop cover in various colors, which some claim is less likely to spook a coyote than one without a cover. As mentioned previously, hunting at night with a light may be illegal.

Many predators, including foxes and bobcats, will approach a distress call. It's also common for a domestic dog to come bouncing in to your call. For this reason, make certain you're a responsible hunter: Positively identify your target before you shoot.

Hunting Over Bait

If you think bait sounds like the perfect solution to getting rid of a troublesome coyote, you're wrong. No bait is sure to lure in a coyote at a convenient shooting time. Bait may or may not bring in a coyote, and if it does, the coyote may come only when you're not there. Nevertheless, if a coyote hits a bait consistently, he could begin taking chances and soon show up in daylight hours when you're there.

Producers and hunters have often set up near dead livestock to wait for a coyote. Although removing a dead sheep, goat,

cow, or horse will decrease the possibility of attracting more coyotes, leaving one in the field could attract a coyote that has
killed livestock. Again, though, it's best to hunt at opportune
times such as early morning and late evening, and set up where
you're least likely to be spotted or scented.

If a dead animal isn't available, consider baiting the coyote
with your own ingredients. This technique can work, particularly near poultry houses where coyotes have killed fowl.

The best ingredients are butcher trimmings—bones, meat
scraps, and fat. Sometimes your local grocery will give you all
you want, or supply it for a reasonable fee. Coyotes dearly love
these trimmings, and won't hesitate to make consistent visits to
a spot once they discover their presence. Coyotes seldom are
hooked on sweets, but they may enjoy the taste of fruits.

While baiting bears, I've often had coyotes come in; however, these baits are not set up to allow any predator to take
what he wants. When setting a coyote bait, you must make certain that Wily will have no problem getting the bait but other
scavengers and smaller predators will have difficulty.

Start the bait with 15 to 25 pounds of trimmings. Place the
bait on the ground and cover it with small logs. The logs should
have a diameter of about 4 to 6 inches and be long enough to
stretch end to end over the bait. Usually, you can round up this
debris close to your bait site. A coyote will finagle his way
through the logs, and in some cases dig under them to get to
the bait. Smaller predators and scavenging birds can't get to the
bait at all.

Before setting the bait, make sure you've selected a location
that provides you with a place to hide while waiting for the coyote to show. Move back as far as possible from the bait, but make

certain you can see it and are within accurate shooting range. Wearing rubber boots and using rubber gloves when handling the logs will reduce human scent that could spoil your hunt. Check the bait every couple of days during midday hours when coyotes are least active, and replenish it as necessary. After you've had several consistent hits, you can begin hunting. Evening hunts are often the most successful, but arrive at least three hours before dusk and wait until darkness to leave.

Hunting with Dogs

Hunting coyotes with dogs has only recently gained popularity, but in areas where open country is abundant, hunters consistently use dogs to harvest coyotes. The dogs run the coyote until it eventually ends up in plain view and within shooting range of the hunter.

Greyhounds are commonly used, as well as various other types of hounds, for hunting coyotes. Some hunters watch open areas for a coyote, and then release the dogs after the sighting. Others release the dogs in prime areas, knowing the dogs will pick up the trail of a coyote. The more fences and brush in the area, the less chance there is that a dog will be effective.

Hunting coyotes with dogs is an effective method for removing coyotes in a given area; however, it may or may not dispose of a particular problem coyote. To locate a group of hunters who use dogs, talk with your local conservation agency. They may know of hunters who would jump at the chance to hunt coyotes with dogs. All you need to do is give permission to hunt on your property.

Although hunting is often an effective means of removing coyotes, it may not target the pest responsible for your damage.

Spot and Shoot

Another popular hunting method is incidental shooting. This is where an individual sets up near an open field and watches for a coyote. Some hunters also use their vehicles to cover as much ground as possible in early morning or late afternoon. Landowners and producers who suffer livestock losses almost always keep their firearm with them when traveling, and make it a point to watch every field and pasture for a coyote. Surprisingly, these incidental kills account for a large portion of the total kills in every state and province.

Nonlethal Traps

When most folks think of trapping, they imagine the animal suffering an agonizing death. This isn't the case. Some suffering may be involved, but most animals are disposed of quickly and painlessly after being trapped. People who do consider trapping an unethical method of controlling coyotes should know that some trapping methods won't cause injury. Products are still being tested, but at least one seems to work well.

When most people think of a nonlethal trapping method, they think of a live box trap. These folks think it would be great to lure Wily into such a trap, and then haul him away to where he'll become a nuisance for someone else. First, let me begin by reminding you of the coyote's cleverness. Any coyote trapper or researcher will tell you that live box traps simply don't work. Most are too small, serving only to catch raccoons and smaller animals. Wily could squeeze into a large live box trap, but he's not that stupid. On the contrary, he's usually difficult to trap when *any* type of trap is used.

In recent years another nonlethal trap has been developed that shows promise. It's called the Collarum. The manufacturer designed this trap strictly for canines. It has, for the most part, been determined safe in urban settings and around livestock. Many folks rely on the device to capture coyotes in backyards, gardens, landfills, pastures, and near poultry houses. The Collarum sends a cable over the head of the coyote and around his neck, holding the animal similarly to how a chain holds a dog.

How effective are the Collarum and other nonlethal traps? In 1998 and 1999 three National Wildlife Research Center biologists conducted tests using several types of nonlethal traps. The 1998 test included an older model of the Collarum, while the 1999 test used the newest. Both tests calculated the effective rates of each trap, and what injuries, if any, a coyote sustained when captured. In addition, the tests showed if the trap caught animals besides coyotes. None of the traps was alike, but each worked by latching onto the coyote's foot, leg, or neck.

Of the animals caught by two of the traps, 70 percent were coyotes; however, the Collarum was particularly selective, with a 100 percent coyote-capture rate. In order for a trap to meet or exceed recently established international standards for humane trapping, at least 80 percent of the animals cannot have injuries. Although each of the traps tested fell short of this standard, the Collarum was close, with 70 percent of the coyotes caught uninjured. Researchers noted that some of the prototypes tested might cause fewer injuries than traditional capture methods but may not be as efficient as other leghold traps. The Collarum had a capture rate of 39 percent, meaning it caught 39 percent of the coyotes it tried to latch onto. Some of the coyotes captured with the device had swelling of the head and neck, and at least four had teeth damage. After the testing, researchers determined the Collarum was much less likely to cause injury and more likely to catch coyotes than those traps that rely on limb restraints. You might be happy to know that it will also result in fewer injuries to dogs.

The Collarum is offered in both a deluxe and a standard model. The deluxe is made of stainless steel (no rusting and low maintenance). See chapter 12 for contact information.

Snaring

Snares are commonly used to catch coyotes, but they work best in certain areas. If you have a fence, a snare can be set up along it to catch a coyote as he walks the perimeter. Snares work best if you have an opening under a fence, or in the fence just above the ground. You can make an opening for a coyote if none exists—but only one. This narrows the field where the coyote will be. Coyotes also travel trails consistently. A snare is often effective when placed along narrow trails where you find dense vegetation along the sides.

A snare is no more than a long steel-cable loop. It will often capture a coyote (and other predators and dogs) by the neck or leg. Rarely, the snare will get around the body of the animal. After you form a loop with the steel cable, place the loop where the coyote must pass through it. You can adjust the cable to make a big or small loop. If there's a threat of snaring a dog, go for a leg snare and use an opening of only 5 inches. To snare a coyote around the neck, use a round or oval 12- to 14-inch loop directly in the opening where the coyote will pass through. The remaining portion of the snare should be wrapped around a support, such as a fence post or a metal post driven into the ground. A swivel in the snare will prevent the cable from twisting. When setting a snare, wear rubber gloves and boots and make certain you aren't brushing against debris. A coyote may detect human scent and avoid the area.

Snares are much simpler to use than leghold traps, and they don't require previous trapping experience. They also cost less than leghold traps and are safer for humans. On rare occasions, livestock and deer are caught in snares. This won't occur if you avoid setting up the snare along a pathway. When a coyote is caught in a snare, you have no choice but to destroy it. Snares should be checked daily.

Steel Leghold Traps

Researchers have noted that leghold traps are the most effective traps for removing problem coyotes. They also claim that these traps have forced coyotes to fear humans in urban as well as rural areas. Some leghold traps are available with laminated or wide rubber jaws; these have proven more humane than older versions, and are less likely to allow coyotes to escape.

Before getting into using a leghold trap, let me first remind you that successful trapping seldom comes with your first attempt. On the contrary, good trappers are rare, and they're skilled experts. They know where and how to set traps for the best results. They also know that one mistake can cost them when pursuing an easy coyote, and that no mistakes can cost them when pursuing a wise coyote. Still, if you've never attempted trapping but have the willingness and the time to get your feet wet, jump on in.

You'll need an array of tools to trap coyotes. Fortunately, you probably have many of them at home. You'll need a 5-gallon bucket to hold your equipment, and a 3-foot-square piece of plastic tarp for kneeling on when you set your trap. A claw hammer will come in handy for driving the 24-inch trap stake into the ground to secure the trap, and it will also dig the holes in the ground that you'll need for your lure and trap. A sifter with small holes (⅛ to ¼ inch) is necessary for sifting dirt back over the trap. You can throw in a curved stick about 1 foot long to level the sifted dirt. Of course, you'll also need to wear rubber gloves and boots to reduce human scent. Add a small piece (a little larger than the trap) of plastic or canvas cloth to your collection. You'll use this to cover your trap pan. Your lure should consist of a bottle of coyote urine, or perhaps another commercial animal scent that will entice the coyote to get in the trap. To soak up your scent when you put it out, take along a 6-inch piece of clean cotton material. For coyotes, most trappers prefer a No. 3 or No. 4 coilspring trap. If you prefer to use a padded-jaw trap, you can try the No. 3 Soft-Catch coilspring trap.

Although some folks might tell you that your traps and other equipment need to be free of rust (they claim that a coyote won't like the smell of rust), this isn't necessarily true. It's true that rust might impede the effectiveness of the equipment, but coyotes don't have a problem with the smell of rust. Think how often coyotes stand next to rusted fences or machinery. If it bothered them, they'd always be running for their lives.

Look for a promising location to set your traps. Usually, these are areas where coyotes frequently travel, such as trails and old roadbeds. Some trappers have success on hilltops where coyotes love to go and howl. Traps shouldn't be set directly on trails or old roadbeds. Instead, set them up on open, level ground alongside the trail or roadbed. Openings are better than thickets, because coyotes spend more time sniffing around these locations than they do the brush that surrounds them. You can also set traps where coyotes have killed livestock or poultry. Coyote tracks and scat provide positive indication of a coyote traveling a particular route (see chapter 6).

Since coyotes frequently travel trails and roads, trappers often set their traps alongside of them.

Choose a dirt-hole or scent-post set, but I'll focus on the dirt-hole set because it's effective and easy. To a coyote, a dirt-hole set looks like a place where another animal buried food.

First, dig a 4-inch-diameter hole about 6 to 8 inches deep at a 45-degree angle. You can do this against a small clump of grass or a piece of log. This serves as a backing. Use your plastic tarp to kneel on, and to store the dirt you dig up. Dig another hole about 1 inch below the ground but wide enough for the trap, about 3 inches in front of the deep hole. Place your trap in this hole after leveling the ground around it. Drive your stake firmly into the ground, and make sure it goes through the swivel on the trap. This will secure the trap to the stake.

Set your trap very carefully to avoid injury. Once the trap is set and level, place the small piece of plastic or canvas over the trap pan and under the trap jaws. To keep the trap from tipping, pack the loose dirt around it to firm the set. Use your sifter to add about ½ inch of soil over the trap. This will cover the trap but won't affect its performance. Finally, level the dirt carefully with the foot-long stick.

To enhance your set, sprinkle a little camouflage around your stake. A clump of grass or a handful of weeds will work. Now add the attractant. In the first hole, place the piece of cotton material and saturate it with a tablespoon of coyote urine or other lure. Instead of using a commercial scent, some trappers use meat scraps from the kitchen table. After dispersing the scent, you must make your deep hole (the one that contains the scent) look as if an animal has buried something. Place some dirt over the scent, as well as a small clump of weeds. Use your stick to add a small mound of dirt around the hole. This makes the hole look as though a critter has partially covered his booty.

There's a lot more tricks to the trade, of course, but these techniques will get you started. They could even trap a coyote.

That's it, other than a little cleanup duty. Smooth the ground around the trap and surrounding area to look like it did before. The coyote is always cautious, but seems to be twice as cautious when he approaches a scent. Before heading off, take one last look around to make certain you didn't leave any tools behind. Take another look around to make certain you didn't place the trap in an area that will endanger any other nontargeted animal. When you walk away, make sure you don't step on your trap or scent hole. Then take a vow to come back every day to check your trap until it's removed.

Although many people oppose the shooting and trapping of coyotes, these lethal methods have been proven to reduce expected damage, and to correct initial damages. The type of control method you use should be based upon the laws governing hunting and trapping in your area as well as your personal preferences.

12

Who You Gonna Call?

QUESTION: *Who should you call if you have a problem with a coyote?*

ANSWER: *I would say the police or the National Guard.*
          —Robbie Williams, age 8

ANSWER: *You should call the army.*
          —Bradley Williams, age 6

T hroughout this book, I've mentioned several control methods to prevent and discourage coyote damage. Additionally, you've heard about several products. This chapter will provide the contact information you need to obtain products or services. However, I haven't disclosed contact information for the army and National Guard.

Wouldn't it be nice if you could make one phone call and hear a helpful voice on the other end: "Coyote Damage Prevention and Control Services. How may I help you get rid of a problem coyote?" I might as well tell you that it isn't that easy, and it may even be difficult to obtain assistance. Get ready to punch a few buttons on the telephone and scratch a few notes. There is no coyote hotline or centralized agency that anxiously awaits your call.

My questionnaire asked each state and provincial wildlife division to name the agency responsible for assisting folks who wanted to report a coyote complaint. Their responses differed considerably, and some could not offer a direct answer. I've listed their comments in the following table.

*Agencies That Handle Most Complaints About Coyotes**

State or Province	Agency to Contact
Arizona	Game & Fish Department
California	USDA Wildlife Services
Florida	Fish & Wildlife Conservation Commission
Georgia	Department of Natural Resources, Wildlife Resources Division, Game Management Section
Idaho	USDA Wildlife Services
Illinois	Department of Natural Resources
Kansas	Kansas State University Research and Extension
Kentucky	Department of Fish & Wildlife Resources and Department of Agriculture
Maine	Inland Fish & Wildlife
Michigan	Department of Natural Resources Wildlife Bureau
Minnesota	Department of Natural Resources
Montana	Department of Livestock handles complaints, but when federal lands are involved, contact USDA Wildlife Services

Agencies That Handle Most Complaints *(Continued)*

State or Province	Agency to Contact
Nebraska	USDA Wildlife Services
New Brunswick	Department of Natural Resources; Department of Agriculture
New York	Department of Environmental Conservation
Northwest Territories	Department of Resources, Wildlife and Economic Development
Nova Scotia	Department of Natural Resources
Ohio	Department of Agriculture and USDA Wildlife Services
Oklahoma	USDA Wildlife Services
Oregon	USDA Wildlife Services
Pennsylvania	Bureau of Dog Law Enforcement handles complaints in some areas
Rhode Island	Fish & Wildlife Division
South Carolina	Department of Natural Resources, Wildlife Management Section
South Dakota	Department of Game, Fish & Parks
Utah	USDA Wildlife Services
Washington	Probably USDA Wildlife Services
West Virginia	USDA Wildlife Services handles sheep problems; Division of Natural Resources handles remaining complaints
Wisconsin	USDA Wildlife Services
Wyoming	USDA Wildlife Services

*As reported by state and provincial wildlife divisions.

The responses listed by these states and provinces are based upon the number and types of complaints they receive, and where the damage occurs. For example, USDA Wildlife Services often assists when coyotes kill livestock, but on the other hand, a state or provincial wildlife agency might help you when Wily kills chickens or pets, or raids the garden in rural areas. These agencies also could direct you to a conservation officer, district biologist, or county agent. In suburbs and urban areas I suggest you first contact your city or county animal damage control agency. In Los Angeles you can contact the County Agricultural Commissioner and Weights and Measures. If human safety is a factor, another agency may respond.

The National Wildlife Research Center functions as an arm of USDA Wildlife Services. Its staff are dedicated to meeting the needs of folks who have experienced wildlife damage. If you need assistance with a problem coyote, feel free to search the archives at www.aphis.usda.gov/ws/. For more information contact:

USDA/APHIS/WS
National Wildlife Research Center
4101 LaPorte Avenue
Fort Collins, CO 80521-2154
Phone: (970) 266-6017
Fax: (970) 266-6010
E-mail: nwrc@usda.gov

Folks in the United States who need federal assistance should contact the USDA office. Since branches are scattered across the country, look for the nearest USDA office in your local phone book under U.S. government agencies.

Commercial assistance may be available when it becomes necessary to remove a troublesome coyote. Some commercial operators work on their own, while others are members of an organization. To find an individual or an organization that will remove a coyote, contact a conservation officer.

Commercial trappers usually work for a fee that depends upon the job. At one time they might have volunteered their services, but today low fur prices have made it impossible for them to make any money unless you find someone who will remove the coyote simply for the outdoor experience and challenge.

If you're looking for guard animals to protect livestock, first consider the species of animal. Sometimes, because of the cost of shipping a large animal, it may be better to start looking close to home. However, you might not find a guard animal nearby.

For guard llamas, contact the following:

Seldom Scene Farm
1710 Watts Ferry Road
Frankfort, KY 40601
Phone: (606) 873-8352
Fax: (606) 873-1622
www.seldomscenefarm.com
E-mail: sscene@lex.infi.net

INCA Llamas
101 Hibbard-Hicks Lane
Willis, TX 77378
www.homestead.com/incallamas/llamasforsale
E-mail: llamas@flex.net

Cedars Edge Llama Farm
1581 270th Street
Diagonal, IA 50845
www.mddc.com/montana/cedar/index
E-mail: montana@mddc.com

For more information about guard dogs and for purchasing a guard dog, contact the following:

Livestock Guard Dog Association
Hampshire College
Box FC
Amherst, MA 01002

The Kangal Dog Club of America, Inc.
P.O. Box 796
Middlebury, VT 05753
Phone: (802) 265-4595
www.turkishdogs.com/kangal
E-mail: KDCA@turkishdogs.com

The Akbash Dog Association of America, Inc.
P.O. Box 796
Middlebury, VT 05753
Phone: (802) 265-4595
www.turkishdogs.com/akbash
E-mail: ADAA@turkishdogs.com

Milk and Honey Farm's Great Pyrenees Dogs
P.O. Box 656
Cokato, MN 55321
www.milkandhoneyfarm.com
E-mail: farm@milkandhoneyfarm.com

Groveland Farm Maremmas Dogs
2862 South Peterson Road
Poplar, WI 54864
www.all-animals.com/groveland/dogs
E-mail: grovland@discover-net.net

Woolger's Willows Farm Akbash Dogs
Box 171
Port Loring, Ontario P0H 1Y0
Phone: (705) 757-0149
www.akbash.net

Before purchasing a guard donkey, you might visit the Web site of the American Council of Spotted Asses at www. spottedass.com, or send e-mail to coreen@wxicof.com. The Web site provides a listing of donkey breeders around the country.

For more guard donkey ads, contact:

Virginia Department of Agriculture and Consumer Services
P.O. Box 1163
Richmond, VA 23218
Phone: (804) 786-3935
Fax: (804) 371-7788
www.vdacs.state.va.us/livestock
E-mail: livestock@vdacs.state.va.us

If you're an educator, particularly of youngsters in a metropolitan area or in the suburbs, you should consider "The Coyote Kit." This kit includes a 30-minute urban coyote video, poster, coyote media file, pamphlets, the Teacher's Guide/Student Activity Manual (120 pages), and more. Students will meet a wildlife biologist, hear about her scientific research, and discuss her problem of assessing attitudes and responses to an increase in urban coyote populations. The kit has a suggested price of $27 (U.S.) and $45 (Canada). For more information contact:

BC SPCA
322–470 Granville Street
Vancouver, BC, Canada V6C 1V5
Phone: (604) 681-3379
E-mail: info@spca.bc.ca

The U.S. Environmental Protection Agency requires special training for certification of M-44 and livestock protection collars containing Compound 1080. For more information contact:

USDA, APHIS, Wildlife Services
4700 River Road
Unit 87
Riverdale, MD 20737
www.aphis.usda.gov

Texas livestock producers can obtain the certification by attending a Texas Department of Agriculture (TDA) Predator Management Training Session. Various licenses are offered. Also available from TDA is publication B-1492 ($10), which is an excellent field guide for determining what type of predator killed your livestock. For more information contact:

Texas Department of Agriculture
1700 North Congress Avenue
Stephen F. Austin Building, 9th Floor
Austin, TX 78701

Phone: (512) 463-7476
Fax: (512) 463-1104
www.agr.state.tx.us

Hunting or trapping a coyote requires an array of equipment. For game calls and other hunting equipment contact:

Nite Lite Co.
P.O. Box 8300
Little Rock, AR 72222
Phone: (800) 648-5483
www.huntsmart.com

Cabela's
400 East Avenue A
Oshkosh, NE 69190
Phone: (800) 237-4444
www.cabelas.com

Bass Pro Shops
2500 East Kearney
Springfield, MO 65898-0123
Phone: (800) 227-7776
www.basspro.com

For trapping supplies contact:

Chagnon's Outdoor World
218 Oak Street
Manistique, MI 49854
Phone: (800) 795-5157
www.trap-supply.hypermart.net

Murray's Lures and Trapping Supplies
Route 1, Box 18A
Elizabeth, WV 26143
Phone: (304) 474-3733
www.murrayslures.com

Otter Creek Lures and Baits
34019 185th Avenue
Stanley, WI 54768
Phone: (715) 447-8779
www.northcoast.com/ottercrk

Water sprayed at high pressure often frightens a coyote. One such device works on a sensor. Contact this company for the ultimate high-pressure sprayer:

Contech Electronics, Inc.
P.O. Box 115
Saanichton, BC, Canada V8M 2C3
Phone: (800) 767-8658
www.scatmat.com

To avoid confusion when attempting to determine if a coyote caused your damage, consider another wildlife damage book I recently wrote. *Nuisance Animals* (softcover, 178 pages, $14.95) covers 40 species of nuisance animals and provides track illustrations, damage identification information, and control methods.

Wild Trails Publishing
6299 Fol-Degonia Road
Tennyson, IN 47637

Phone: (812) 567-8948
www.wildtrails.com
E-mail: wildtrails@psci.net

For frightening devices, such as lights, noisemakers, and exploders, contact one of the following companies:

DeerBusters
9735 A Bethel Road
Frederick, MD 21702
Phone: (888) 422-3337
www.deer-busters.com

Nasco
901 Janesville Avenue
Fort Atkinson, WI 53538-0901
Phone: (800) 558-9595
www.enasco.com

The Positive Side of Wily

13

The Positive Side of Wily

QUESTION: *What are some of the good things about coyotes?*

ANSWER: *They will get rid of rotten food in your garden.*
—Jessica Webster, age 12

My conscience finally caught up with me. Since 50,000 of the 70,000 words in this book have been dedicated to negative facts about coyotes, it's finally time to say something good about our friendless adversary. Besides, who can blame Wily and the rest of his comrades for the dirty deeds that we should be held responsible for?

Coyotes have expanded their range, but primarily because we eliminated larger predators. As human populations continue to boom, every person needs a place to live, food to eat, and a long list of resources. Nevertheless, the construction of more homes and industrial sites, and the exploitation of more resources are only part of the reason why coyotes are causing us problems. Consider how many roads we have today. Consider how many more are on the way. Consider how the boundaries of our cities keep inching their way into the countryside. Yep, coyotes can't help but live alongside humans. Coyotes must go somewhere. Sometimes it's the middle of a wilderness at least 100 miles from the nearest burger joint. Sometimes it's your backyard.

Now that I have the "who's to blame" over with, I'll get on with the positive side of coyotes. First, it would not hurt to admire the coyote for his ability to contend with humankind's progress. Many species of North American mammals haven't been so fortunate. Some animals are still abundant today, but only because humans lent them a helping hand. Coyotes did it without our help. They did it despite the war we declared on them many decades ago.

Now let's take just one more look at the coyote's remarkable and cunning ability to survive. You have to wonder how there can be so many coyotes, yet so few of them in sight. After all, there are more of them today than ever before, and we're now sharing habitat. I can't help but admire the coyote for his ability to remain hidden, despite his expansion.

And can we ignore the coyote's talents in the music circuit? As far as I know, he's never enjoyed the standing ovations that the Beatles and Elvis earned. Nonetheless, if ever a day comes that we can't set up camp in the West and hear his mystical howls, we will have lost something essential to our well-being. We will have also lost the song that once inspired western pioneers and Indians. It's nice to know that on the right day the coyote's romantic serenade can still be heard almost anywhere.

Some folks have implied that the coyote is a worthless hunk of flesh and hide that has only cost us money. While he has cost the taxpayer more money than the IRS took in last month, he has also made money for us. Consider the cost of film and processing. As a wildlife photographer, I have shot more than a few rolls of film and have contributed more than a few dollars to Kodak and Fuji. Other photographers have contributed many more dollars, not to mention those few thousand tourists that have exercised their index finger on the shutter of a camera.

But the economic value of Wily goes much further. The coyote's hide has become a cherished souvenir for some. Hunters and trappers have sought his hide for centuries. Coyote pelts are not nearly as valuable as they once were, but it doesn't stop hunters and trappers from pursuing this challenging predator. They have spent millions on licenses and equipment to have this opportunity. Has it slowed the coyote's expansion? What a foolish question. I couldn't come up with any statistics that showed how many coyotes are taken annually by hunters and trappers, but one report shows that Nebraska hunters took 540,000 coyotes in that state alone from 1941 to 1989.

As I've mentioned previously in this book, the coyote despises the fox. Foxes were introduced to America during the mid-1700s as prey for hounds and hunters. Only recently in Orange County, California, red foxes were attempting to eliminate a couple of native endangered coastal birds along one of the few coastal wetlands left in that county. Before coyotes moved into the area, the foxes were preying heavily on light-footed clapper rails and least terns. One report indicated that a single red fox could prey on more than 40 newly hatched least tern chicks in one night. The reason for the massive killing goes back to the habits of the red fox. He doesn't always stop and devour what he kills on location. Instead, he kills all he can and stores it up to feed on later.

Researchers in Orange County now believe that a small population of coyotes (the new predators on the block) will decrease the number of endangered birds being preyed upon by foxes. Yes, coyotes will snatch a few of the endangered birds, but they also feed on other mammals and vegetation. The red fox falls into the "other mammals" category.

Many animals capitalize on the coyote's prey. Consider all of the scavenging animals and birds that stroll across the remains of a carcass after a coyote fills his stomach. Ravens, crows, eagles, foxes, bears, martens, and many more critters have enjoyed a few leftovers compliments of Wily. Nature does a superb job of making certain nothing goes to waste. Coyotes are simply part of nature's scheme.

We've also talked about coyotes preying upon game animals, but you'll have a difficult time trying to find text in this book that says the coyote has annihilated a particular species. Some research indicates that the coyote has, in rare instances, been responsible for decreases in animal populations, but for the most part, he hasn't. Coyotes usually feed on big game animals, such as deer, when the population needs to be reduced, or when Old Man Winter weakens them. It's also safe to assume that coyotes do help keep some animal populations from exploding. Out-of-control colonies of rodents might be climbing the walls in your house right now if it weren't for predators such as Wily.

When animal populations are reduced, it usually makes someone happy. Take the woodchuck, which has created oodles of problems for farmers and livestock producers. These varmints dig numerous holes and create hazards for livestock. They also eat cash crops. After the coyote arrived in some areas, woodchuck numbers declined. Groundhogs and groundhog hunters hated it, but the farmers and livestock producers loved it.

Every animal including Wily serves a purpose in nature's scheme. Here, he helps keep the rodent population from exploding.

In some northern states, nesting ducks have their best chance of survival when coyotes are present. Foxes feed consistently on nesting ducks, and other animals grab them when opportunity allows. Wily won't turn down a free duckling either, but he also feeds on other predators, which will sometimes increase the population of ducks.

I regret that I cannot come up with any more positive remarks about Wily. Maybe you can. If so, I commend you. The coyote ranks at the bottom of the list with many folks, and he needs all the help he can get. As for me, I feel a little guilty after coming up with only 1,500 positive words. However, I do have more respect for the coyote than I did 70,000 words ago.

If all the beasts were gone, men would die from a great loneliness of spirit, for whatever happens to the beasts also happens to the man . . .

—Chief Seattle of the Suwamish Tribe

Bibliography

Andelt, William F., Robert L. Phillips, Kenneth S. Gruver, and Jerry W. Guthrie. "Coyote Predation on Domestic Sheep Deterred with Electronic Dog-Training Collar." *Wildlife Society Bulletin* 27 (1), Spring 1999.

Baker, Rex O., and Robert M. Timm. "Management of Conflicts Between Urban Coyotes and Humans in Southern California." *Proceedings, 18th Vertebrate Pest Conference.* Edited by Rex O. Baker and A. Charles Crabb. University of California, Davis, 1998.

Bodenchuk, M. J., J. R. Mason, and W. C. Pitt. *Economics of Wildlife Damage.* Fort Collins: Colorado State University Press, 2001.

Burns, Richard J., Doris E. Zemlicka, and Peter J. Savarie. "Effectiveness of Large Livestock Protection Collars Against Depredating Coyotes." *Wildlife Society Bulletin* 24 (1996): 123–127.

Cadieux, Charles L. *Coyotes: Predators and Survivors.* Washington: Stone Wall Press, 1983.

———. *Pronghorn, North America's Unique Antelope.* Harrisburg, PA: Stackpole Books, 1986.

Carbyn, Ludwig N. "Coyote Attacks on Children in Western North America." Canadian Wildlife Service, *Wildlife Society Bulletin* 17 (1989): 444–446.

Gese, Eric M., and Scott Grothe. "Analysis of Coyote Predation on Deer and Elk During Winter in Yellowstone National Park, Wyoming." *American Midland Naturalist* 133 (1995): 36–43.

————, Robert L. Ruff, and Robert L. Crabtree. "Intrinsic and Extrinsic Factors Influencing Coyote Predation of Small Mammals in Yellowstone National Park." *Canadian Journal of Zoology* 74: 784–797, in collaboration with the University of Wisconsin, 1996.

Green, Jeffrey S., and Roger A. Woodruff. "Livestock Guarding Dogs Protecting Sheep from Predators." U. S. Department of Agriculture, APHIS, Agriculture Information Bulletin Number 588, July 1999.

Henke, Scott E., and Fred C. Bryant. "Effects of Coyote Removal on the Faunal Community in Western Texas." *Journal of Wildlife Management* 63 (4): 1066–1081.

Knowlton, Frederick F., Eric M. Gese, and Michael M. Jaeger. "Coyote Depredation Control: An Interface Between Biology and Management." *Journal of Range Management* 52 (5), September 1999.

Lampa, Kristine. "Urban Coyotes in the Lower Mainland, British Columbia: Public Perceptions and Education." Master's thesis, University of British Columbia, 1997.

MacCracken, James G. "Coyote Foods in a Southern California Suburb." *Wildlife Society Bulletin* 10 (1982): 280–281.

Meadows, Laurie E., and Frederick F. Knowlton. "Efficacy of Guard Llamas to Reduce Canine Predation on Domestic Sheep." *Wildlife Society Bulletin* 28 (3), fall 2000.

Parker, G. R. "The Seasonal Diet of Coyotes in Northern New Brunswick." New Brunswick: Canadian Wildlife Service, 1986.

Parker, Gerry. *Eastern Coyote.* Halifax: Nimbus Publishing, 1995.

Rue, Leonard Lee III. *Complete Guide to Game Animals.* New York: Outdoor Life Books, 1981.

Shivik, John A., Kenneth S. Gruver, and Thomas J. DeLiberto. "Preliminary Evaluation of New Cable Restraints for Capturing Coyotes." *Wildlife Society Bulletin* (forthcoming).

U.S. Department of Agriculture. *Effective Wildlife Services Projects Factsheet.* Wildlife Services, Animal Plant Health Inspection Service, December 1997.

————. *Prevention and Control of Wildlife Damage.* University of Nebraska Cooperative Extension, Institute of Agriculture and Natural Resources, University of Nebraska—Lincoln, Animal and Plant Health Inspection Service, Animal Damage Control, Great Plains Agricultural Council, 1994.

————. *Wildlife Services Program Highlights, Fiscal Year 1999.* Animal Plant Health Inspection Service, Miscellaneous Publication No. 1564.

Young, Stanley P., and Hartley H. T. Jackson. *The Clever Coyote.* Harrisburg, PA: Telegraph Press, 1951.

Zaidle, Don. *American Man-Killers.* Long Beach, CA: Safari Press, 1997.

Index

279

Jaeger, Michael M., 26, 28, 83, 87, 200, 220
Jasper National Park (Canada), 117, 119

Kangal Dog Club of America, Inc., The, 262
kangaroo rats, 158, 159
Knowlton, Frederick F., 166, 200
  on coyote behavior, 26, 28, 83, 87
  on llamas, 202, 203
  predation study of, 121, 220

Lampa, Kristine, 90, 92, 102, 191–92, 193
Langlois, Susan, 100
lighting, as frightening device, 227–28
Livestock Guard Dog Association, 262
livestock losses, 5, 15, 57–58, 63, 73
  economic costs of, 78–84, 220
  predation patterns and, 139, 141–42
  protecting livestock with guard animals, 199–217
  supplemental protection, 219–38
livestock protection collars (LPCs), 230-32

llamas, as guard animals, 199, 200-205, *206,* 207, 261–62
Lyme disease, 183–85
lynx, 131

M-44 ejectors, 232, 264
MacCracken, James, 67, 69
Mason, J. R., 59, 82, 122
Mason, Russ, 161
Meadows, Laurie E., 202, 203
melons, coyotes' fondness for, 89–90, 149, 194
Milk and Honey Farm's Great Pyrenees Dogs, 262
minks, 148–49
monogamy, 35
Morill, Bill, 103
mountain lions, 80, 84, 127, 204
  bounties on, 162
  donkeys and, 215
  guard animals and, 202
  predation patterns of, 144
  tracks of, 131
music, as frightening device, 227, 237

National Agricultural Statistics Service, 81, 82
National Wildlife Research Center, 260
Native Americans, 2, 5